Artist Bubbles Chocolate Dolphin Eskir

Zoo

arn

ylophon

Vikin

Umbrella

iger

Snowman

Rainbow Quilt Panda Ostrich Needlework

minaa

Garden

Hippo

Inchworm

Jackpot

Kite

Lollipop

Music

Cross-Stitch from A to Z

designs by

Linda Gillum

for
Kooler Design Studio

Bobbie Matela.........................MANAGING EDITOR
Carol Wilson Mansfield............................ART DIRECTOR
April McArthur..............................EDITOR, BOOK DESIGN
Carly Poggemeyer ....................CONTRIBUTING EDITOR
Sandy Scoville ....EDITORIAL ASSISTANT
Christina Wilson.............................EDITORIAL ASSISTANT
Wendy Mathson ....GRAPHIC DESIGNER

Photographed models stitched by:
Melissa Cahill, Linda Causee,
Bonnie Chancellor, Barbara Chancy,
Jessica Chism, Betty Curran,
Maryann Donovan, Millie Fortner,
Connie Gallegos, Ellen Harnden,
Sandi Kardack, Janet Kazmer,
Sue McVae, Maxine Meadows,
Mary Alice Patsko, Carly Poggemeyer,
Lee Ann Tibbals, Christina Wilson,
Nancy Withrow.

Cross-Stitch Charts by:
Rick Causee, Barbara Chancy,
Lisa DeLasaux, Patti C. Galliano,
Carly Poggemeyer, Brent Rathburn,
Glenda Tucker, Christina Wilson.

For a full-color catalog including books of cross-stitch designs, write to:

American School of Needlework™
Consumer Division
1455 Linda Vista Drive
San Marcos, CA 92069

Or visit us at **www.asnpub.com**

Our thanks to Coats & Clark, Charles Craft, Zweigart
and Crafter's Pride for supplying materials for use in this book.

©2003 Kooler Design Studio, Inc.
Published by American School of Needlework, Inc.; ASN Publishing
1455 Linda Vista Drive, San Marcos, CA 92069

ISBN: 1-59012-059-0   Printed in U.S.A.   All rights reserved.   23456789

Introduction

What fun! From talented designer Linda Gillum, and the Kooler Design Studio, come dozens of delightful cross stitch designs – several for each letter of the alphabet.

Alligator and Dinosaur, Gymnast and Jellies, Puppies and Parachute, Slippers and Seal, these and all of our charming characters will dance off the pages and onto your favorite cross stitch fabric or perforated paper.

A cuddly little bear hugs the letter beginning each chapter – perfect for monograms and remembering birthdays. Each chart is color-coded and cross-referenced for Anchor or DMC floss to make stitching a breeze.

We've decorated bookmarks and bottles, clothing and coasters, fridgies and frames, placemats and pajamas to help stir up your own ideas for gift-giving.

So pick a letter, choose a design, and let's begin.

3

Table of Contents

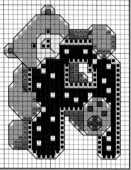

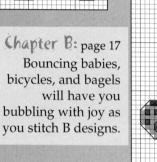

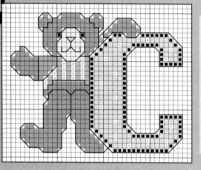

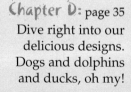

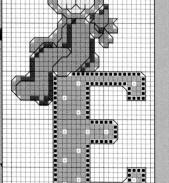

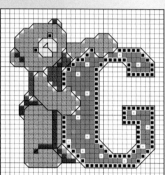

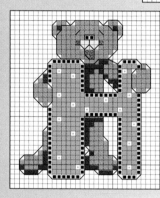

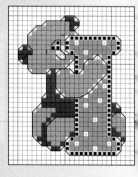

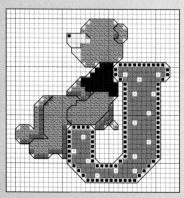

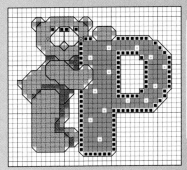

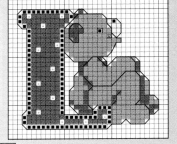

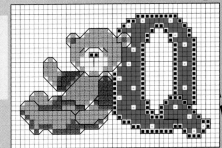

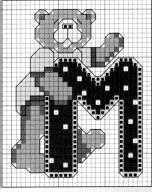

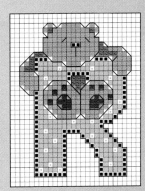

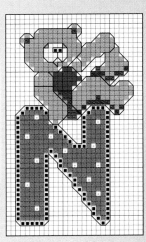

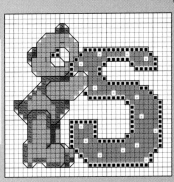

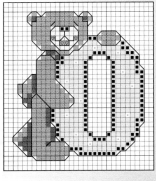

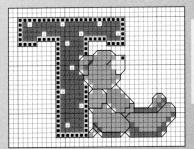

Table of Contents (continued)

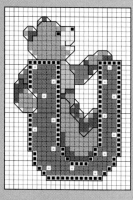

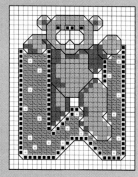

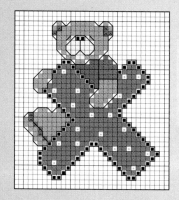

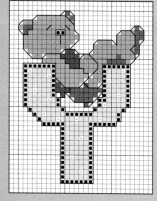

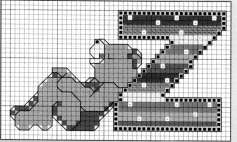

A is for...

Archer
Artist
Anchor
Armor
Ape
Acorn
Armadillo
Antelope
Alligator
Apple on a Stick
Apple Pie
Apple
Ants
Alarm Clock
Armchair
Asleep
Ark
Airmail
Airplane

Anchor	DMC
2	blanc
387	712
334	606
881	945
1047	402
1048	3776
351	400
403	310

Backstitch:
351—bear (except
eyes, nose)
403—"A," eyes, nose

7

A is for...

Archer

Artist

Anchor

Armor

Anchor	DMC		Anchor	DMC
2	blanc		146	322
387	712		361	738
334	606		369	435
313	742		881	945
323	722		1047	402
311	676		1048	3776
305	743		1049	301
204	563		234	762
128	775		399	318
159	3325		400	317
129	809		403	310
161	813			

French Knot: 403
Backstitch:
334—artist's brush handle, duck's shirt stripes
210/562—archer's grass
146—artist's smock stripes
162/825—bird (except leg & beak)
351/400—armor bear (except eyes, nose, mouth), archer bear (except eye, nose, mouth), artist bear (except eye & nose), brush, bird leg & beak, hive, easel legs
1049—duck feet & beak, rope
400—remaining duck (except eye), duck's hat & remaining shirt, armor's suit, armor's flag, bow, arrow, target, artist's remaining smock, canvas
403—duck's eye & anchor; amor's eyes, nose, mouth, & flag pole; archer's bow, arrow, nose, eye, mouth, and glasses; artist's hat eye, nose, & bee

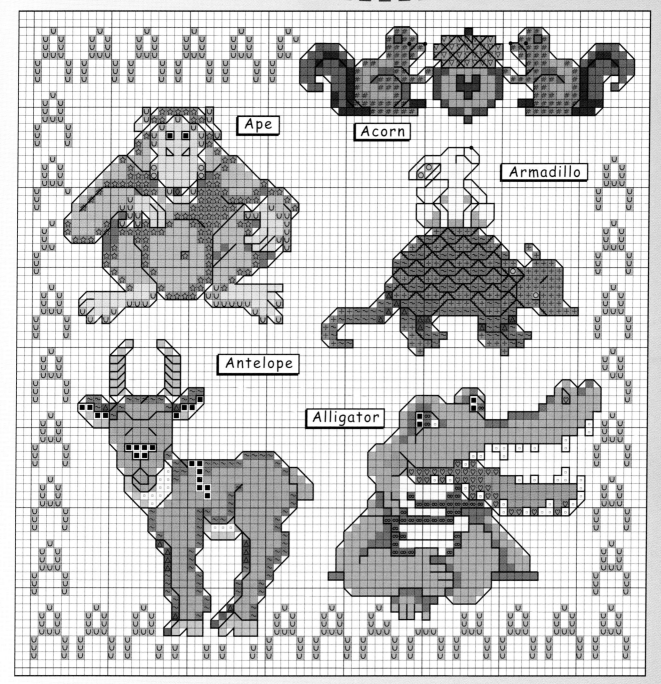

	Anchor	DMC		Anchor	DMC	French Knots:
▫	2	blanc	▣	146	322	38—rabbit's nose
☐	885	739	✛	881	945	403—squirrels' eyes & noses
▣	74	3354	~	347	402	**Backstitch:**
◯	36	3326	△	349	301	38—rabbit's inner ear
◈	38	961		351	400	349—remaining rabbit
♡	76	3731	✳	1047	402	351—squirrels, acorn, antelope (except antlers,
■	334	606	▣	1048	3776	eyes, nose, mouth, hooves), alligator's
☐	4146	950	▣	390	3033	chin folds
U	9575	3779	▽	1080	842	936/632—armadillo (except eye)
▣	361	738	☆	1082	841	1086—ape (except eyes, nose, mouth)
∞	891	676	▣	1086	839	400/317—alligator (except eyes), antelope's
▣	363	436	▣	234	762	antlers & hooves
▣	842	3013	▣	399	318	403—ape's eyes, nose, mouth; alligator's eyes;
▣	843	3053	■	403	310	armadillo's eye; antelope's eyes, nose, mouth

Apple on a Stick

Apple Pie

Ants

Apple

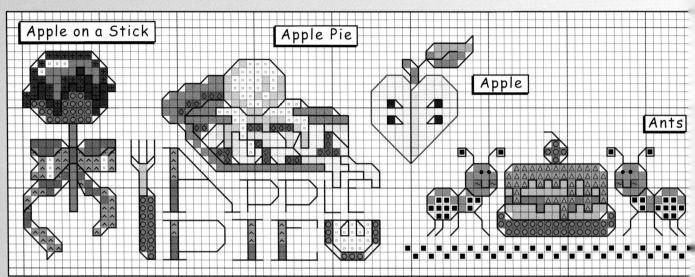

Apple on a Stick

Apple Pie

Apple

Ants

Anchor	DMC	Anchor	DMC
2	blanc	240	966
885	739	128	775
25	3326	129	809
334	606	146	322
47	321	347	402
778	3774	369	435
882	758	349	301
884	356	936	632
311	676	399	318
259	772	403	310

French Knots: 403

Backstitch:
334 (2 strands)—heart apple outline
884—cake, cherry stem
210/562—heart apple leaf, leaf stem
146—lettering
349—heart apple center line & stem
351/400—pie
936—heart apple seeds, apple slice seeds
400/317—ice cream, fork, remaining
    apple slice, candy apple, bow
403—ants, cake plate, cherry

Anchor	DMC		Anchor	DMC
2	blanc	◇	204	563
387	712		209	913
36	3326		128	775
334	606	+	129	800
47	321		146	322
311	676		347	402
314	741	∧	881	945
292	3078	☆	1047	3954
~	295	726	■	403	310
206	564			

French Knots: 403
Backstitch:
38/961—clock mouth
130/809—chair stripes
146—pillow, "zzz"
884/356—clock eyebrows
351/400—bear (except face)
403—bear face, clock eyes
400/317—remaining outlines

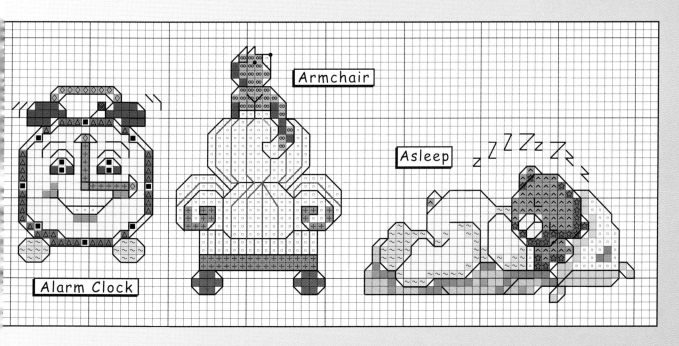

Armchair

Asleep

z Z Z Z z Z z Z

Alarm Clock

A is for... Ark

Anchor	DMC	Anchor	DMC	French Knots: 403
2	blanc	129	809	**Backstitch:**
73	963	146	322	39—heart
75	962	109	209	877—"AND THE ANIMALS CAME TWO
39	309	368	437	BY TWO"
4146	950	1047	402	146—waves
361	738	1048	3776	351/400—alphabet, giraffes, ark roof
305	743	388	842	shingles, foxes (except ears & tails), fish
185	964	234	762	400/317—elephants, sheep, clouds,
877	501	399	318	raccoons, flamingos, fox ears & tails,
128	775	403	310	remaining ark

14

A is for... Airmail

Airplane

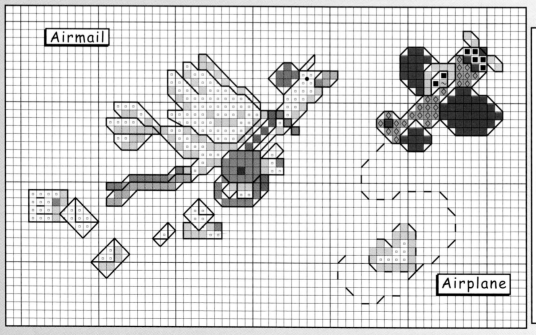

Airmail

Airplane

Anchor	DMC
2	blanc
334	606
868	758
323	722
326	720
128	775
145	809
146	322
347	402
369	435
351	400
403	310

French Knot: 403
Backstitch:
146—hat, vapor trail
351—mailbag, beak, collar, legs
400/317—remaining bird, letters, airplane

16

B is for...

Ball
Blocks
Baby Bottom
Bubble Bath
Balloon
Baby & Bottle
Baby
Best Friends
Bubbles
Beaver
Backpacker
Bicycle
Baker
Bagel
Bumble Bear
Barrel
Binoculars

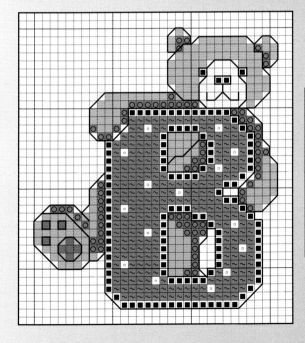

Anchor	DMC
2	blanc
387	712
329	3340
351	400
881	945
1047	402
403	310

Backstitch:
351—bear (except eyes, nose, mouth)
403—eyes, nose, mouth, "B"

17

B is for...

Baby Bottom
Blocks
Ball
Bubble Bath
Balloo[...]

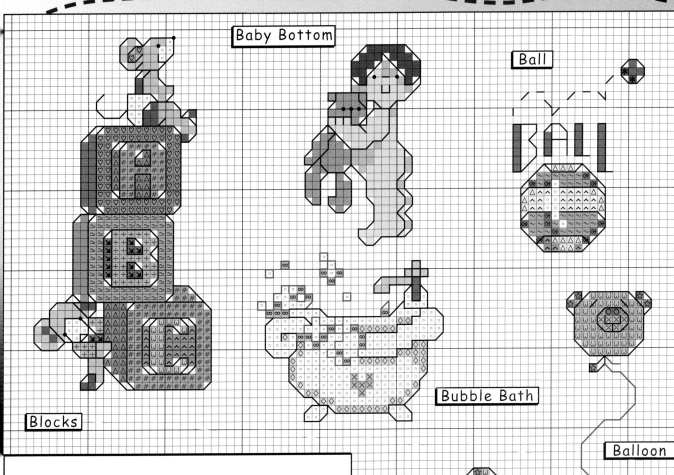

Baby Bottom

Ball

Blocks

Bubble Bath

Balloon

Anchor	DMC	Anchor	DMC
2	blanc	1043	369
24	963	206	564
74	3354	205	912
76	961	1092	959
29	309	185	964
334	606	159	3325
47	321	161	813
1012	754	1031	3753
868	758	128	775
6	761	130	809
9	352	146	322
328	3341	342	211
300	745	108	210
301	744	109	209
302	743	884	356
366	951	234	762
311	676	399	318

French Knots: 403/310
Backstitch:
35/3705—bottle baby's mouth, bear
  baby's mouth
29—balloon
1006/304—"BALL"
884—bottle baby's skin & hair, nipple, ball
  baby's skin & hair, bear baby's nose &
  skin, bear (except nose)
146—balloon string, bubbles
400/317—bottle baby's clothes, remaining
  bottle, balls, bounce line, ball baby's
  clothes, mice, blocks, tub, faucet
403—bear's nose

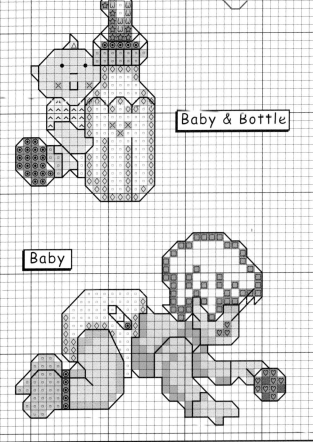

Baby & Bottle

Baby

Best Friends

Bubbles

Beaver

Anchor	DMC		Anchor	DMC
2	blanc	⊠	129	800
885	739		146	322
24	963		1080	842
334	606		1084	840
301	744		881	945
361	738	⌃	1047	402
206	564		391	303
204	563	⊙	392	642
1031	3753	■	403	310

French Knots: 403

Backstitch:

334—bear's shirt stripes

210/562—frog (except eyes, mouth), log leaves

145/809—bubbles

146—"BEST FRIENDS"

349/301—rabbit (except face)

351/400—bears (except eyes, noses, mouths)

1086/839—log, beaver (except nose, teeth), dog (except nose)

400/317—rabbit's face, bubble wand, bear clothes

403—dog's nose & mouth; frog's eyes & mouth; beaver's nose & teeth; bears' eyes, noses, mouths

B is for...

Anchor	DMC		Anchor	DMC
334	606		1086	839
47	321		881	945
1012	754		1047	402
842	3013		234	762
844	3012		399	318
129	809		235	414
146	322		403	310
883	3064			

French Knots: 403
Backstitch:
35/3705—boy's mouth
883—boy's skin, staff
351/400—bear (except face)
400/317—bike, clothes,
                    bed roll, tools
403—bear's face, boots, pack

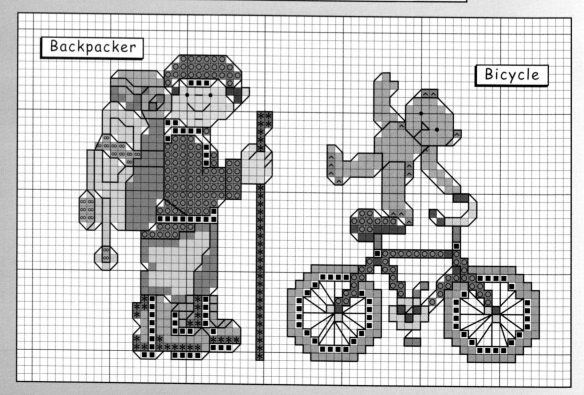

Backpacker

Bicycle

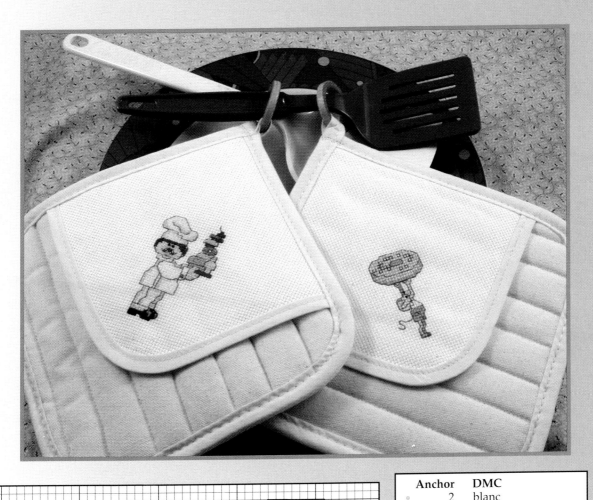

Bagel

Baker

Anchor	DMC
○ 2	blanc
□ 885	739
23	3713
46	666
1012	754
♡ 868	758
295	726
~ 362	437
1031	3753
☆ 130	809
146	322
881	945
✳ 883	3064
936	632
1047	402
234	762
∧ 399	318
■ 403	310

French Knots: 403
Backstitch:
1006/304—cherry
351/400—bagel, chef's
    remaining food, chef's skin
936—hair, mustache
400/317—mouse, chef's clothes
    (except shoes)
403—chef's shoes

B is for...

Bumble Bear   Binoculars   Barrel

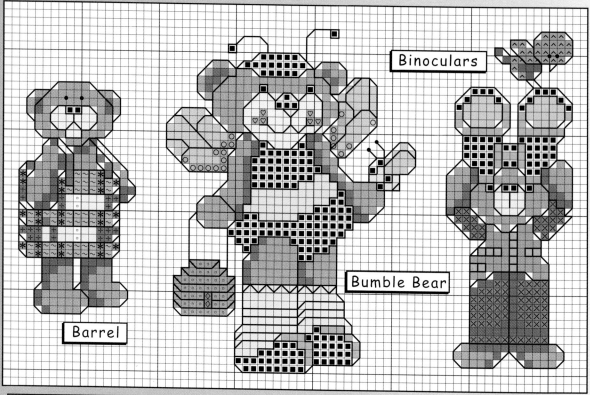

Binoculars

Bumble Bear

Barrel

	Anchor	DMC			Anchor	DMC
▫	2	blanc		⌃	129	809
	387	712			146	322
♡	23	3713		◇	351	400
	295	726			881	945
▫	361	738			1047	402
✛	891	676		~	391	303
	852	3047		✳	392	642
✕	854	371			1086	839
	856	370			234	762
	1031	3753		■	403	310
○	144	800				

French Knots: 403
Backstitch:
146—bird (except beak & legs), wings
351—bee bear (except eyes, nose, mouth), hive, barrel bear (except nose & mouth), binocular bear (except nose), bird beak & legs
1086—barrel, straps
400/317—binoculars, binocular bear's clothes
403 (2 strands)—bee bear's hat antennae
403—binocular bear's nose, barrel bear's nose & mouth, bee body, bee bear's hat, eyes, nose, mouth, & clothes

C is for...

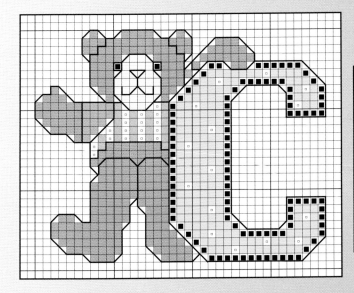

Anchor	DMC
2	blanc
387	712
303	742
240	966
108	210
881	945
403	310

Backstitch:
351/400—bear (except
eyes, nose, mouth)
403—eyes, nose, mouth,
shirt, "C"

C is for...

Cats

Caterwaul

Catnap

Anchor	DMC		Anchor	DMC
2	blanc	∪	347	402
387	712		211	562
1021	761		185	964
74	3354		140	3755
1023	3712	∧	96	3609
334	606		98	553
1012	754		378	841
313	742		234	762
323	722	✕	399	318
328	3341		400	317
324	721	■	403	310

French Knots: 403
Backstitch:
1025/347—singing cat nose
334—left "CATS"
1006/304—white cat nose
211—frame, blue-green "CATS"
147/797—blue "Cats"
99/552—purple "CATS"
351/400—sleeping cat (except eyes, nose, mouth),
top sampler cat (except eyes & nose), smiling
sampler cat (except mouth)
400—singing cat (except eyes, nose); siamese, red
collar cat, gray cat, and white cat (all except
eyes, noses, and mouths)
403—"zzz," musical notes, remaining sampler cats,
remaining eyes, noses, mouths, pawprints

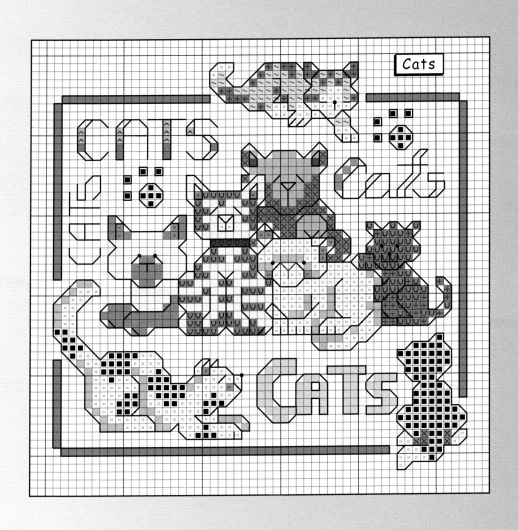

Cats

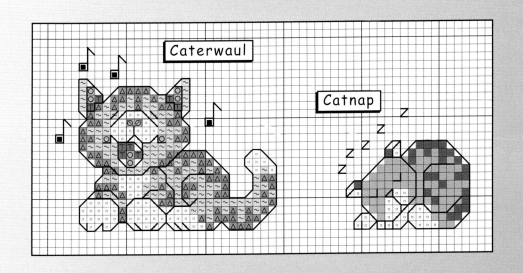

Caterwaul

Catnap

C is for...

Anchor	DMC		Anchor	DMC
387	712		379	3772
24	963		1084	840
241	966	~	881	945
129	809		1047	402
146	322		399	318
376	3774	■	403	310

French Knots: 403
Backstitch:
1086/839—chocolate bar
1049/301—bears (except eye & noses)
400/317—chocolate bear's clothes
403—shoes, leotard, motion lines,
     noses, eye

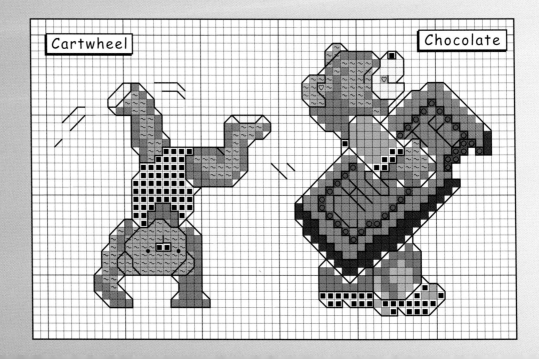

Cartwheel

Chocolate

Anchor	DMC
2	blanc
334	606
96	3609
98	553
295	726
1043	369
129	809
146	322
108	210
110	208
347	402

French Knots: 400/317
Backstitch:
334—shirt stripes
334 (2 strands)—hanger
—bloomer stripes
351/400—clothes pins
400—clothesline,
   remaining clothes

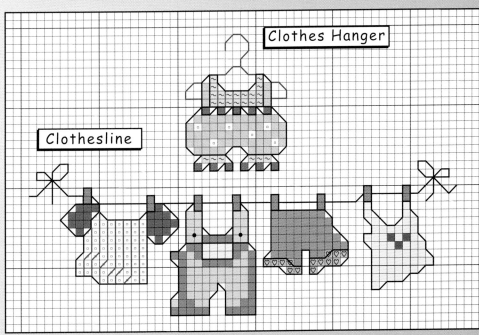

Clothes Hanger

Clothesline

is for...

Couch Potato

Cowboy

Curls

	Anchor	DMC		Anchor	DMC
▫	2	blanc		363	436
	275	746		241	966
♡	24	963		210	562
◉	334	606	⊞	1092	964
	47	321		186	959
	96	3609		1031	3753
~	778	3774		129	809
◈	868	758		108	210
⌃	6	754	∿	347	402
	328	3341		349	301
	295	726		234	762
△	361	738	■	403	310

French Knots: 403
Backstitch:
334—"chips"
47—cowboy's mouth, girl's mouth
147/797—"couch potato"
349—girl's skin & hair, cowboy's skin
351/400—potato (except eyes), chip, chip bag;
   cowboy's hair, belt, & rope
400/317—cowboy's hat, shirt, & chaps;
   potato's chair, ottoman, glass, hat & slippers,
   girl's clothes; bear (except nose)
403—cowboy's boots, bear's nose, potato's eyes
403 (2 strands)—cowboy's & girl's eyes

30

Anchor	DMC
2	blanc
334	606
778	3774
301	744
361	738
210	562
130	809
366	951
347	402
349	301

French Knots: 403
Backstitch:
47/321—cat's nose, boy's mouth
146/322—water
349—remaining cat, boy's skin & hair, inside canoe
400/317—remaining canoe, oar, clothes, hat
403/310—boy's eyes

Canoe

Anchor	DMC		Anchor	DMC
2	blanc		204	563
23	3713		211	562
25	3326		1031	3753
334	606		1049	301
313	742		234	762
329	3340		399	318
302	743		403	310
1043	369			

French Knot: 403
Backstitch:
211—leaves
884/356—bell, cow's face (except eye)
1049—branch, bird's beak
400/317—remaining bird
403—remaining cow, collar

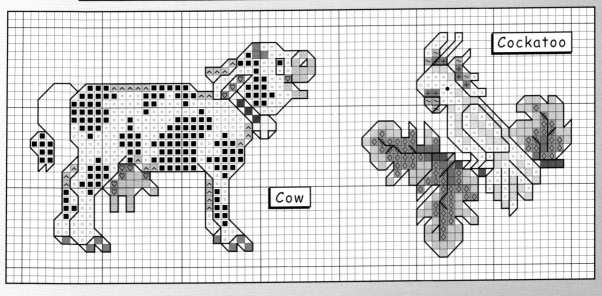

Cockatoo

Cow

Anchor	DMC
2	blanc
334	606
47	321
96	3609
98	553
778	3774
329	3340
295	726
306	783
129	809
146	322
349	301
234	762
235	414
403	310

Backstitch:
47—nose, mouth
351/400—crown (except fur trim), hair, skin
400/317—car, fur trim, clothes, shoes
403—eyes

Crown

Car

D is for...

Doctor
Dance
Dive
Dust
Dinosaurs
Dragon
Dogs
Dig
Dolphins
Duck

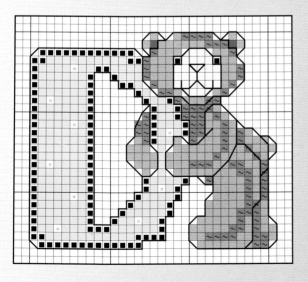

Anchor	DMC
2	blanc
387	712
295	726
881	945
1047	402
1048	3776
403	310

Backstitch:
351/400—bear (except eyes, nose, mouth)
403—eyes, nose, mouth, "D"

D is for...

Doctor   Dance   Dive   Dust

Doctor

Dance

Dust

Dive

Anchor	DMC		Anchor	DMC		Anchor	DMC
2	blanc		302	743		1047	402
933	543		311	676		1048	3776
48	3689		204	564		399	318
74	3354		206	563		235	414
76	961		1092	964		403	310
333	608		186	959			
334	606		128	775			
778	3774		129	809			
868	758		146	322			
1012	754		342	211			
323	722		347	402			
313	742		349	301			
300	745		1086	839			
301	744		881	945			

French Knots: 403

Backstitch:

76—dancer's clothes, mouth, necklace

47/321—diver's mouth, duster's mouth

1013/3778—diver's skin & hair, dancer's skin
& hair, doctor's skin, child's skin

351/400—doctor's hair, bear (except face),
child's hair

1049/301—cat, duster's hair & skin

349—cat's muzzle and mouth

400/317—diver's cap & suit, doctor's clothes,
shoes, stethoscope, child's clothes, stool,
duster, motion lines, duster's clothes
(except stockings & boots)

403—diver's eyes, bear's face, doctor's eye,
duster's eyes, stockings & boots

D is for...

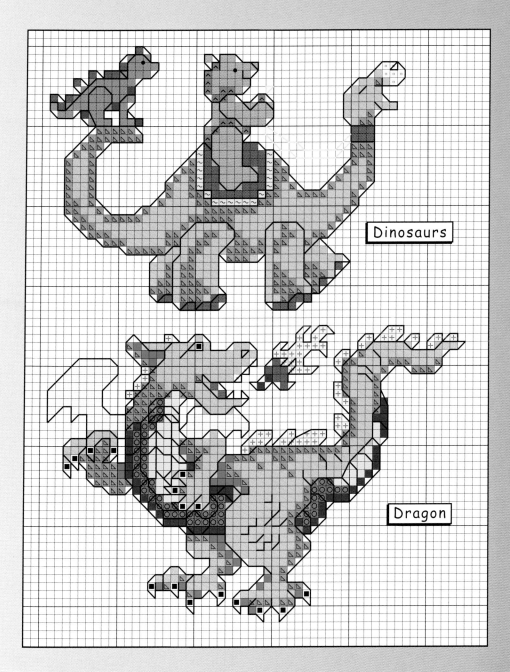

Dinosaurs

Dragon

Anchor	DMC	Anchor	DMC	
2	blanc	1043	369	**French Knots:** 403
275	746	241	966	**Backstitch:**
1024	3328	210	562	—reins
333	608	167	519	211/562—green scales
328	3341	168	807	351/400—bear (except nose & mouth),
314	741	108	210	wings, flames, chest & belly scales
298	972	881	945	400/317—dinosaurs (except eye),
305	743	1047	402	remaining dragon (except eye), saddle
311	676	403	310	403—bear's nose & mouth, dinosaur's
				eye, dragon's eye

D is for...

Dogs

Anchor	DMC		Anchor	DMC
2	blanc		914	407
387	712		367	738
1021	761		347	402
1023	3712		884	356
334	606		899	3782
1006	304		234	762
259	772		848	927
211	562		399	318
147	797		403	310
378	841			

French Knots: 147
Backstitch:
1023—tongue crease
1006—"DOG!"
147—remaining lettering, pawprint
369/435—bone
236/3799—dogs (except eyes &
     noses), balls, bounce lines, wag
     lines, bone hanger, leash, Yorkie
     ribbon, bulldog collar
403—eyes, noses

D is for...

Dig

Dolphins

Duck

Anchor	DMC
2	blanc
387	712
24	963
96	3609
314	741
206	564
240	966
209	913
185	964
120	3747
140	3755
108	210
881	945
1047	402
370	434
391	303
392	642
403	310

French Knots: 403

Backstitch:

211/562—leaves

1049/301—duck's beak & feet, tree trunk

393/640—dirt, bone

400/317—dolphins (except eye), dog (except eye & nose), remaining duck (except eye), inner tube

403—eyes, nose

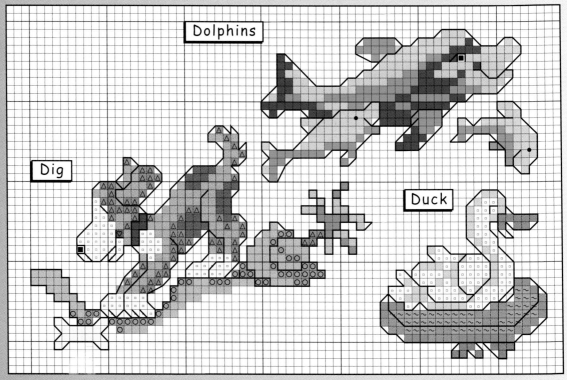

Dolphins

Dig

Duck

E is for...

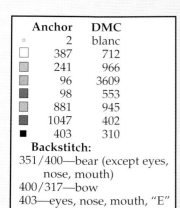

Anchor	DMC
2	blanc
387	712
241	966
96	3609
98	553
881	945
1047	402
403	310

Backstitch:
351/400—bear (except eyes, nose, mouth)
400/317—bow
403—eyes, nose, mouth, "E"

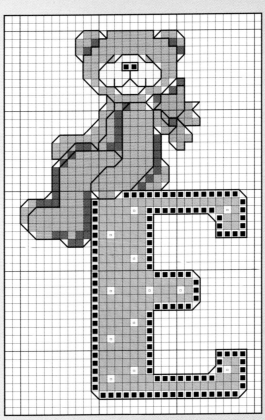

E is for...

Anchor	DMC
2	blanc
388	842
74	3354
334	606
778	3774
868	758
300	745
301	744
305	743
1043	369
241	966
211	562
167	519
168	807
128	775
96	3609
98	553
914	407
1007	3772
234	762
399	318
403	310

French Knots: 403
Backstitch:
47/321—bulb filament,
   Eskimo's mouth
305 (2 strands)—light glow lines
211—cord, plug
1007—Eskimo's nose
351/400—bulb base
400/317—mouse, mouse's
   clothes, slippers, outlet,
   bulb, Eskimo's clothes,
   doll, seal (except eye, nose,
   mouth)
403—seal's eye, nose, & mouth,
   Eskimo's eyes, light cord
   hook

Eskimo

Electricity

44

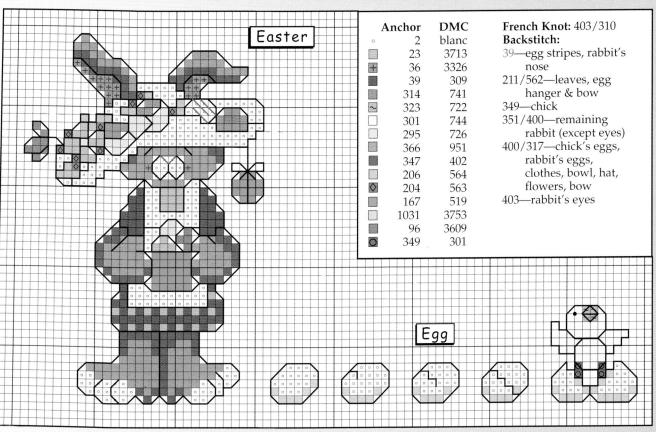

Easter

Anchor	DMC	French Knot: 403/310
2	blanc	**Backstitch:**
23	3713	39—egg stripes, rabbit's
36	3326	nose
39	309	211/562—leaves, egg
314	741	hanger & bow
323	722	349—chick
301	744	351/400—remaining
295	726	rabbit (except eyes)
366	951	400/317—chick's eggs,
347	402	rabbit's eggs,
206	564	clothes, bowl, hat,
204	563	flowers, bow
167	519	403—rabbit's eyes
1031	3753	
96	3609	
349	301	

Egg

E is for...

Exercise

Egghea

Anchor	DMC		Anchor	DMC		Anchor	DMC
2	blanc		136	799		1049	301
387	712		95	554		899	3782
74	3354	^	96	3609		397	3042
1031	3753		109	209	~	398	415
O 129	809		881	945		235	414
▽ 140	3755	✕	1047	402	■	403	310

French Knots: 403
Backstitch:
131/798—water
351/400—bear (except nose & mouth)
393/640—glasses

400/317—book, mole (except nose & mouth), elephant (except eye)
403—bear's clothes, mole's & bear's nose & mouth, elephant's eye

Elephant

Exercise

Egghead

F is for...

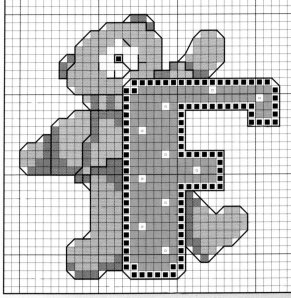

Anchor	DMC
2	blanc
387	712
256	704
95	554
97	553
881	945
1047	402
403	310

Backstitch:
351/400—bear (except eyes, nose, mouth)
400/317—shirt
403—eyes, nose, mouth, "F"

F is for...

Flamenco Dancer

Flamingo

Flamenco Dancer

Flamingo

Anchor	DMC	
2	blanc	
334	606	
778	3774	
8	353	
35	3705	
323	722	
204	563	
185	964	
187	958	
128	775	
880	951	
882	758	
398	415	
399	318	
403	310	
701	(muliné lamé)	

French Knots: 403

Backstitch:
334—hair flower
1013/3778—flamenco
    dancer's skin & face
11/351—flamingo (except
    beak & legs)
901/680—comb (except teeth)
211/562—fan flower stems
884/356—flamingo's legs
400/317—flamingo's beak &
    bow, dress, fan, castanet
403—hair, stockings, shoes
701—comb teeth, earring

F is for...

Friends Forever

Fox

Feed

Fetch

Anchor	DMC		Anchor	DMC
2	blanc	☐	129	809
387	712	◉	136	799
24	963	▦	146	322
1024	3328	~	368	437
334	606	▦	349	301
778	3774	◇	881	945
303	742	▦	1047	3856
301	744	☆	1048	402
305	743	▦	1049	3776
361	738	▦	234	762
363	436	■	403	310
204	563			

French Knots:
1024/3328—pawprint
403—eyes

Backstitch:
1024—cat's nose & mouth, friend dog's tongue
47/321—fetch boy's mouth, feed boy's mouth
146—lettering, ball motion lines
131/798—bird (except beak & legs)
349—friend dog (except nose & muzzle)
351/400—bone, dog food, feed boy's skin, fetch boy's skin & hair, fetch dog (except nose &

mouth), ball, bird's beak & legs, fox (except inner ears, nose, mouth, legs)
936/632—feed boy's hair
400/317—feed dog (except eye & nose), feed boy's clothes & shoes, spoon, cans, fetch boy's clothes & shoes, remaining cat, fetch dog's collar

Backstitch:
403—feed dog's eye & nose; fetch boy's eyes; fetch dog's nose & mouth; friend dog's nose & muzzle; fox's inner ears, nose mouth, legs, paws

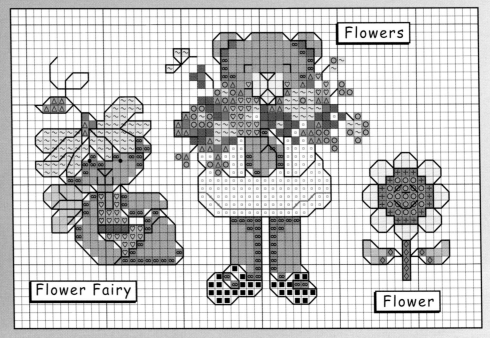

Flowers

Flower Fairy

Flower

Anchor	DMC	Anchor	DMC
2	blanc	240	966
387	712	209	913
75	962	210	562
35	3705	1031	3753
323	722	96	3609
330	947	881	945
302	743	1047	402
305	726	1049	301
203	564	403	310

French Knots: 403
Backstitch:
1006/304—flower's mouth
1098/606—fairy's dress
211/561—all leaves & stems
136/799—wings
146/322—girl bear's dress
    stripes
1007/3772—flower's petals
    & nose

351/400—fairy (except nose
    & mouth), fairy's
    flower, girl bear (except
    face)
400/317—girl bear's dress
    & face (except eyes)
403—fairy's nose & mouth;
    flower's eyes; girl
    bear's eyes, shoes,
    butterfly

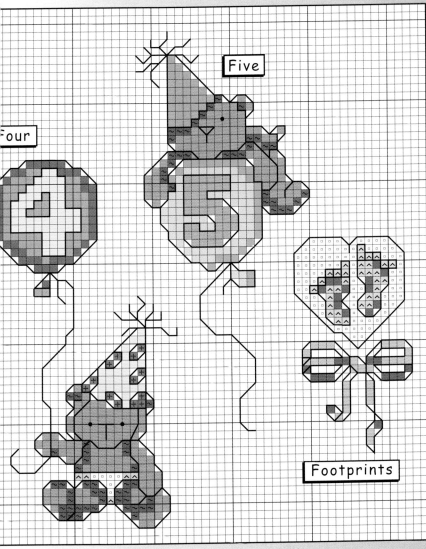

Five

Four

Footprints

Anchor	DMC
2	blanc
36	3326
38	961
334	606
305	743
254	3348
255	907
160	827
161	813
1031	3753
144	800
96	3609
881	945
1047	402

French Knots: 403/310
Backstitch:
39/309—heart, bow
334—four bear's hat streamers, five bear's balloon string
146/322—footprints
98/553—five bear's hat streamers
351/400—bears (except noses)
400/317—four bear's balloon string & balloon, diaper, remaining hats, five bear's balloon
403—noses

F is for...

Fishing

Fish

Float

Anchor	DMC		Anchor	DMC
2	blanc		129	809
334	606		136	799
778	3774		146	322
868	758		96	3609
314	741		1086	839
332	946		881	945
301	744		1047	402
367	738		1049	301
842	3013		391	303
843	3053		392	642
204	563		399	318
240	966		403	310
226	703			

French Knot: 403
Backstitch:
47/321—boys' mouths
1013/3778—float boy's hair & skin,
    fish boy's skin
845/730—fish boy's hat & boot cuff
204—fishing line
146—water, bubbles
351/400—fish (except eye)
1086—fish boy's hair & stump
400/317—float boy's clothes & float,
    fish boy's vest, shirt, pants, rod
    & reel
403—all eyes, fish boy's boots &
    hook

Garden
Grandfather
Grandma
Girl
Guitar
Graduate
Goalie
Gymnast
Golf
Golashes
Girdle
Giraffe
Groundhog

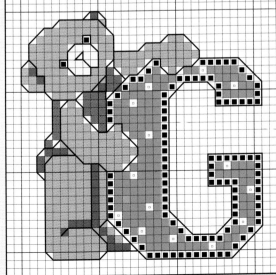

	Anchor	DMC
▫	2	blanc
☐	387	712
▨	225	703
▨	109	209
▨	881	945
▨	1047	402
■	403	310

Backstitch:
351/400—bear (except
 eyes, nose)
400/317—shirt
403—eyes, nose, "G"

G is for...

Garden

Anchor	DMC		Anchor	DMC
2	blanc		225	703
885	739		204	563
74	3354		210	562
334	606		217	561
1006	304		167	519
778	754		1031	3753
868	738		129	809
1008	3773		146	322
1007	3772		96	3609
313	742		99	552
329	3340		388	842
326	720		1048	3776
301	744		376	3774
305	743		378	841
361	738		234	762
891	676		235	414
253	472		403	310

French Knots: 403
Backstitch:

47/321—boy's mouth

217—lettuce in corner; basket vegetables; all stems, leaves, & vegetable tops; green check borders

146—clouds, bee wings, bird (except beak & legs)

936/632—rust border, pumpkin in border, sun, boy's hair & skin, hat, bird's beak & legs; plant stake, rake handle, corn ears, rabbit (except nose & mouth), dirt, carrots in corner

403—remaining bees, ladybug, butterfly, boy's eyes, rabbit's nose & mouth

400/317—remaining outlines

56

Garden

G is for...

Grandfather

Grandma

Grandfather

Grandma

	Anchor	DMC
▫	2	blanc
♡	74	3354
■	76	961
◉	334	606
□	778	3774
~	868	758
■	328	3341
■	1043	369
■	240	966
▫	186	959
□	1031	3753
■	130	809
■	342	211
■	882	950
■	234	762
■	399	318

French Knots:
42/956—Grandma lettering
146/322—Grandfather lettering
403/310—eyes

Backstitch:
42—Grandma lettering,
  heart, mouths
187/958—apron stripes
146—Grandfather lettering
884/356—skin, baby's hair
400/317—chair,
  Grandfather &
  Grandma hair, clothes,
  shoes, sign line
403—eyes
701 (2 strands muliné
  lamé)—glasses

Girl

Guitar

Graduate

Goalie

Gymnast

Golf

Anchor	DMC		Anchor	DMC
▫ 2	blanc		⬖ 225	703
⊠ 73	963		■ 217	561
♡ 74	3354		+ 185	964
■ 76	961		□ 1031	3753
⊙ 334	606		⌃ 129	809
◨ 1005	816		■ 146	322
□ 778	3774		■ 96	3609
~ 868	950		■ 882	758
□ 301	744		◲ 1008	3773
☆ 305	743		■ 884	356
□ 306	783		△ 392	642
■ 842	3013		■ 234	762
■ 843	3053		■ 235	414
□ 253	472		■ 403	310

French Knots: 403

Backstitch:

39/309—girl's mouth

334—goalie's lettering, graduate's sock stripes, girl's hearts & lettering

217—golfer's pant stripes

884—graduate's hair & skin, guitar boy's skin & stool

1007/3772—goalie's hair, skin & stick; golfer's hair & skin, girl's hair & skin, gymnast's hair & skin

393/640—guitar boy's hair

400/317—goalie's clothes (except gloves) & mask; graduate's cap, robe, diploma, remaining socks & shoes; guitar boy's clothes & guitar; golfer's hat, clothes, shoes, club, & ball; girl's clothes & shoes; gymnast's clothes & bar

403—goalie's eyes & gloves, guitar boy's glasses & shoes, golfer's eyes

G is for...

Golashes Girdle Giraffe Groundhog

Anchor	DMC
2	blanc
387	712
74	3354
334	606
297	973
361	738
928	3761
168	807
1031	3753
342	211
109	209
881	945
1047	402
1048	3776
351	400
391	303
392	642
234	762
399	318
403	310

French Knots:
351—giraffe's horn
905/3021—groundhog's eye
403—remaining eyes, girdle grommets

Backstitch:
169/806—lettering
98/553—groundhog's hat stripes
351—giraffe (except nose), bear (except nose & mouth)
905—groundhog
400/317—groundhog's remaining hat, hippo (except eye), girdle (except laces)
403—giraffe's skates; hippo's eye; girdle laces; bear's nose, mouth, & boots

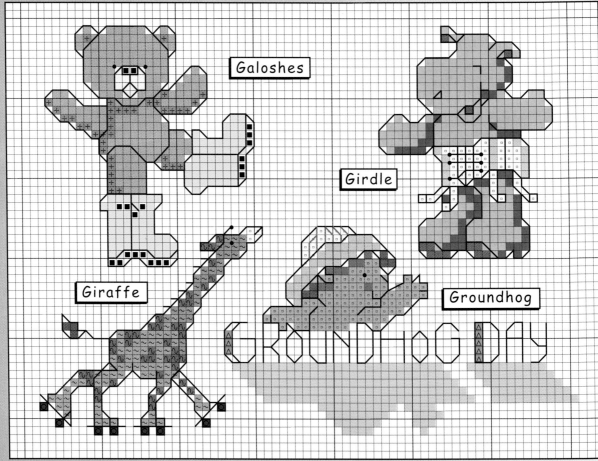

Galoshes

Girdle

Giraffe

Groundhog

H is for...

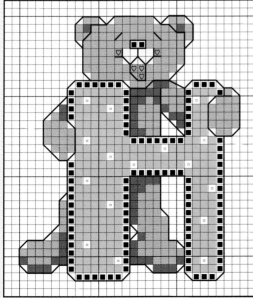

Anchor	DMC
2	blanc
387	712
24	963
186	959
881	945
1047	402
403	310

Backstitch:
351/400—bear (except eyes, nose, mouth)
403—eyes, nose, mouth, "H"

63

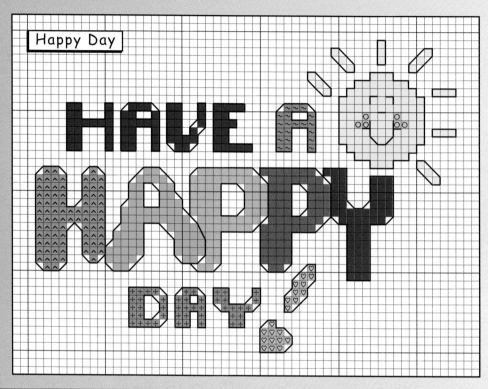

Happy Day

Anchor	DMC		Anchor	DMC
73	963		225	703
334	606		185	964
8	353		145	809
329	3340		96	3609
301	744		98	553

Backstitch:
42/326—mouth, exclamation point
349/301—nose, sun outline, sun rays
400/317—lettering
403/310—eyes

Anchor	DMC		Anchor	DMC
2	blanc		203	564
73	963		145	809
334	606		367	437
1005	816		1047	402
313	742		1048	3776
300	745		234	762
361	738		403	310
362	729			

French Knots:
1005—"HOME," "FRIEND"
146/322—remaining lettering, paw prints
403—eyes
Backstitch:
334—roofs
1005—"HOME," "FRIEND"
146—remaining lettering, paw prints
884/356—cat (except muzzle), dog (except muzzle)
403—dog muzzle, checked portions of houses
400/317—remaining outlines

Home

H is for...

Hop

Hydrant

Hedgehog

Hatch

Hug

Hippo

Hedgehog

Hatch

Hop

Hippo

Hug

Hydrant

Horse

Anchor	DMC		Anchor	DMC
2	blanc		129	809
387	712		146	322
24	963		95	554
334	606		388	3842
1006	304		1084	840
323	722		881	945
301	744		1047	402
361	738		884	356
362	437		391	3782
1042	504		392	642
203	564		234	762
240	966		399	318
226	703		403	310
1031	3753			

French Knots: 403

Backstitch:

211/562—dino (except backplates & eye)

884—rabbit (except nose), horse (except eye, mane, tail, hooves)

351/400—bears (except eyes & noses)

393/640—bear's pant stripes

1086/839—hedgehog (except eye & nose)

400/317—hippo (except eye), rabbit hop lines, horse hooves, dino backplates & eggshell, bears' clothes, shoes, hydrant, dog (except eyes), collar

403—horse eye, mane, tail; hippo eye; hedgehog; dino, bear's eyes, nose & belt; dog eyes; rabbit, hedgehog

H is for...

Helicopter

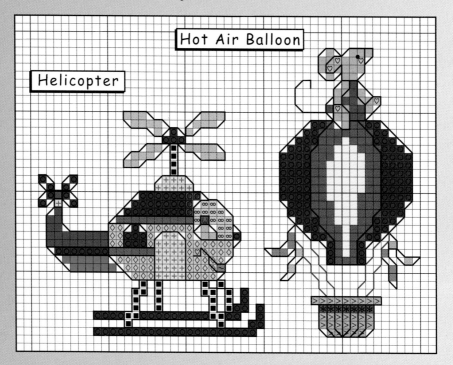

Hot Air Balloon

Helicopter

Anchor	DMC		Anchor	DMC
♡ 24	963		130	809
∼ 76	961		⬩ 145	799
● 334	606		146	322
329	3340		108	210
☐ 295	726		110	208
⊞ 311	676		▷ 881	945
206	564		✳ 1047	402
225	703		234	762
◇ 185	964		399	318
∞ 1031	3753		■ 403	310

French Knot: 403
Backstitch:
334—rope lines
209/913—green flag
146—blue flags
110—purple flag
1049/301—basket
400/317—mouse, balloon, helicopter (except eye, propeller shaft, & runner legs)
403—eye, propeller shaft, runner legs

Anchor	DMC
2	blanc
334	606
778	3774
868	758
305	743
300	745
311	677
891	676
206	564
1031	3753
130	809
95	554
349	301
234	762

Backstitch:
42/326—mouth
145/809—bee wings
1007/3772—hair, skin
349—hive, bee bodies (except
  stripes)
400/317—clothes, chair, spoon
403/310—bee stripes, antennae,
  baby's eyes

Highchair

Hive

H is for...

Home Sweet Home

Home Sweet Home

Anchor	DMC		Anchor	DMC
2	blanc		1031	3753
885	739		130	809
25	3326		146	322
1013	3778		96	3609
328	3341		351	400
332	946		881	945
301	744		1048	3776
305	743		388	842
1042	504		234	762
203	564		235	414
241	966		400	317
210	562			

French Knots:
146—lettering
403/310—flag pole, fences

Backstitch:
1025/347—sun's mouth
212/561—bushes
146—lettering, clouds, bird in tree
351—trees, sun (except eyes & mouth), roof shingles, siding, door mat
400 (2 strands)—decorative trim over door
400—remaining house (except roof fence & weathervane), flag, flagstones
403—sun's eyes, remaining birds, weathervane, flag pole, fences

	Anchor	DMC
▫	73	963
♡	76	961
~	95	3609
◯	97	554
⤢	334	606
◼	1005	816
▢	9	352
⊞	323	722
☐	305	743
T	302	742
+	254	3348
U	203	564
▦	225	703
▦	185	964
▤	128	775
◈	145	809
▦	108	210
>	96	3609
▦	98	553
ꙟ	881	945
▦	1047	402
■	403	310

French Knots: 403
Backstitch:
2/blanc (2 strands)—hat pin
1005—red roses
210/562—first hat bow, second
    hat leaves
211/561—bear hat leaves, stems
349/301—orange roses
400/317—first hat, middle hat,
    middle stand, third stand,
    bear (except nose), sweater
403—first hat stand, third hat,
    bear's hat & nose

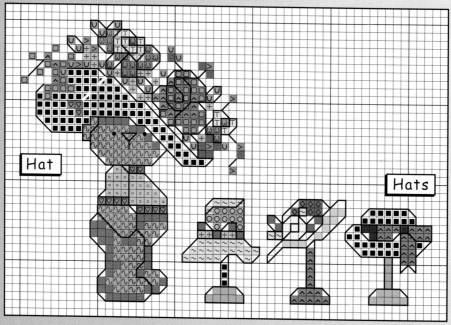

Hat

Hats

I is for...

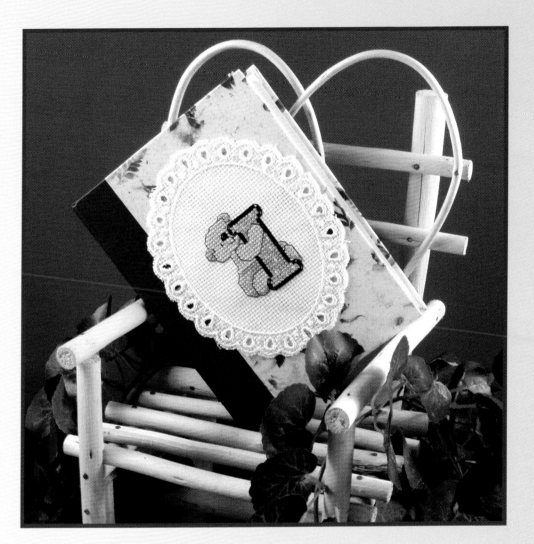

Anchor	DMC
2	blanc
387	712
129	809
95	554
881	945
1047	402
403	310

Backstitch:
351/400—bear (except eyes, nose, mouth)
400/317—shirt
403—eyes, nose, mouth, "I"

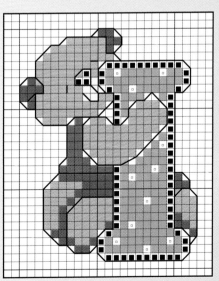

I is for...

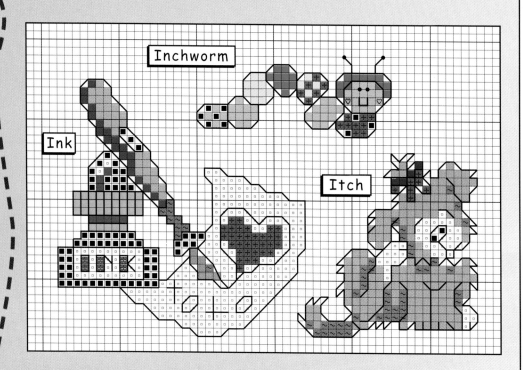

Inchworm

Ink

Itch

Anchor	DMC
2	blanc
24	963
334	606
1006	304
302	743
311	676
253	472
225	703
128	775
130	809
361	738
1047	402
234	762
235	414
403	310

French Knots:
334—worm antennae
403—worm eyes

Backstitch:
334—worm mouth, antennae
1005/816—"INK"
1049/301—paper, pen tip
884/356—dog (except eyes, nose, mouth)
400/317—remaining pen, ink bottle lid ridges, dog's bow
403—remaining ink bottle; heart; Xs, Os; remaining worm; dog's eyes, nose, & mouth

Anchor	DMC		Anchor	DMC		Anchor	DMC
2	blanc		209	913		1047	402
885	739		167	519		1048	3776
24	963		128	775		1049	301
26	894		145	809			
334	606		342	211			
85	3609		882	758			
778	3774		884	356			
328	3341		936	632			
206	564		881	945			

French Knots: 403/310
Backstitch:
42/326—strawberry ice cream, boy's mouth
209—boy's shirt stripes

145—ice cubes, water, pillow, sheets, ruffle, thermometer
884—remaining ice cream, cone
351/400—bed, bear (except face)
1049—boy's hair & skin
400/317—chair, clothes, ice bowl, boy's glasses, toy bear (except face), quilt
403/310—boy's eyes, bears' faces

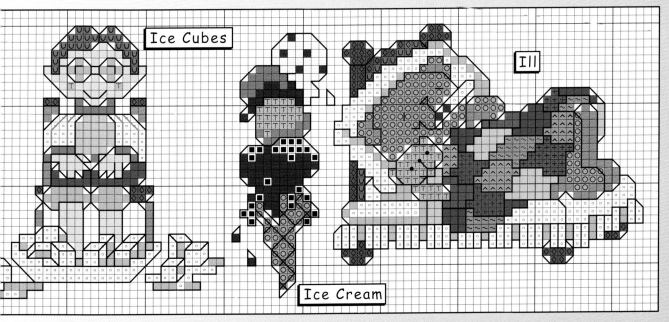

Ice Cubes

|||

Ice Cream

:I is for...

Ice Skater

Anchor	DMC
2	blanc
778	3774
300	745
311	676
1092	959
161	813
128	775
146	322
95	554
109	209

Backstitch:
29/309—mouth
110/208—skirt
884/356—hair, skin
400/317—remaining
   clothes, skates
403/310—eyes

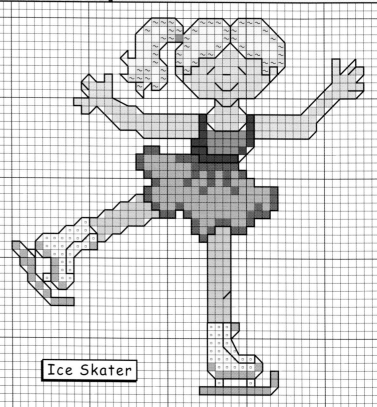

Ice Skater

J is for....

Jump
Javelin
Joy
Junior
Janitor
Jam
Jellies
Jackpot
Jar
Juggle
Jeans
Jaguar

Anchor	DMC
2	blanc
387	712
24	963
334	606
136	799
881	945
1047	402
403	310

Backstitch:
351/400–bear (except eye, nose, mouth)
400/317–shirt
403–eye, nose, mouth, "J"

J is for...

Javelin

Jump

Joy

Janitor

Junior

Anchor	DMC		Anchor	DMC
2	blanc		217	561
387	712		128	775
24	963		129	809
334	606		146	322
1006	304		108	210
329	3340		110	208
301	744		881	945
361	738		1047	402
302	743		234	762
311	676		398	415
1002	977		399	318
204	563		403	310

French Knots: 403

Backstitch:

351/400—all bears (except faces), broom, candleholder, dad's glasses, flame, wick

400/317—candle bear's clothes, candle, joy bear's shirt (except smile face), janitor's clothes, trash can, javelin bear's clothes javelin

403—all faces, dad's & junior's remaining clothes (except pinstripes), smile face

Backstitch:

400—suit pinstripes

Anchor	DMC		Anchor	DMC	French Knots: 217/561
2	blanc		1002	977	**Backstitch:**
334	606		254	3348	334—middle jar tie, "Jellies"
47	321		260	772	hearts
103	211		241	966	1005/816—"JAM"
96	3609		128	800	217—leaves, grasshopper
778	3774		129	3325	146—outer jar ties
8	3824		130	809	884—boy's skin & hair,
11	351		146	798	grasshopper branch, coins
323	3825		342	554	400/317—grasshopper jar,
329	3340		109	209	boy's clothes, shelf, all jam
301	744		884	356	jars & lids, "Jam" heart
305	743		399	318	403—boy's eyes, jam & jellies
311	3827		403	310	borders, pot, "JACKPOT"

Jam   Jellie   Jar   Jackpot   JACKPOT

Juggle

Jeans

Anchor	DMC
2	blanc
334	606
96	3609
778	3774
868	437
302	743
311	676
203	564
225	703
129	809
146	322
347	402
1084	840
403	310

Backstitch:

334—jean boy's shirt stripes

147/797—jean cuffs

884/356—all skin, jean boy's hair

1086/839—juggler's hair

400/317—jean boy's clothes & shoes, juggler's balls & shoes

403—jean boy's eyes; juggler's socks, eyes, & clothes

J is for...

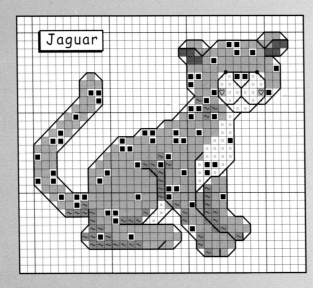

Jaguar

Anchor	DMC
2	blanc
24	963
361	738
882	758
883	3064
403	310

French Knots: 403
Backstitch:
351/400—jaguar
(except face)
403—face

K is for...

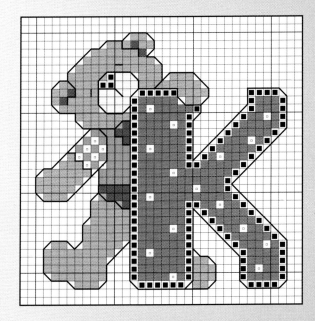

	Anchor	DMC
▫	2	blanc
□	387	712
▨	240	966
▨	97	554
▨	881	945
▨	1047	402
■	403	310

Backstitch:
351/400—bear (except
    eyes & nose)
400/317—shirt
403—eyes, nose, "K"

Kimono

King

	Anchor	DMC
▫	2	blanc
☐	275	746
◇	48	3689
♡	55	604
	57	602
︿	24	963
⊞	26	894
◉	334	606
■	1005	816
☐	778	3774
～	868	758
▫	303	742
⊠	323	722
☐	301	744
☆	302	743
	254	3348
◇	226	703
	209	913
	1092	3811
℧	186	959
△	1031	3753
	342	211
	109	209
■	403	310

French Knots:
1006/304—chopsticks
403—eyes

Backstitch:
57—kimono lady's mouth,
   rabbit's nose & mouth
334—staff bow
1006—chopsticks
302 (2 strands)—robe chain
211/562—lettuce
349/301—crown, chair, staff,
   chain buttons
1007/3772—kimono lady's
   skin
400/317—umbrella (except
   handle), kimono,
   remaining rabbit,
   rabbit's clothes
403—kimono lady's eyes,
   hair, shoes, umbrella
   handle

K is for...

	Anchor	DMC			Anchor	DMC
□	2	blanc		◇	225	703
♡	24	963			168	807
■	334	606			129	809
+	85	3609		▲	136	799
◎	87	3607			108	210
	778	3774			883	3064
~	868	758		▨	884	356
⌃	313	742		∿	1082	841
✕	323	722		∞	1084	840
□	301	744		■	403	310
☆	305	743				

French Knots: 403

Backstitch:

334—kid 4 shirt stripes, kid 5 shoe tips

1006/304—kids 2-4 mouths, kid 4 pink flower

209/913—kid 3 collar stripes

146/798—inner sign's border

884—kids 1, 2, 4 skin & hair, kid 3 skin & flower, kid 1 mouth

1086/839—kid 3 hair, kid 5 skin & hair

400/317—kid 1 clothes (except collar & cuff) & shoes, kid 2 clothes, kid 3 clothes & shoes, kid 4 clothes (except headband & shoes, kid 5 clothes & shoes, sign outline, handprint, lettering (except crayon)

403—kid 1 collar & cuff, kid 2 shoes, kid 4 headband, crayon, remaining eyes

Kindergarten

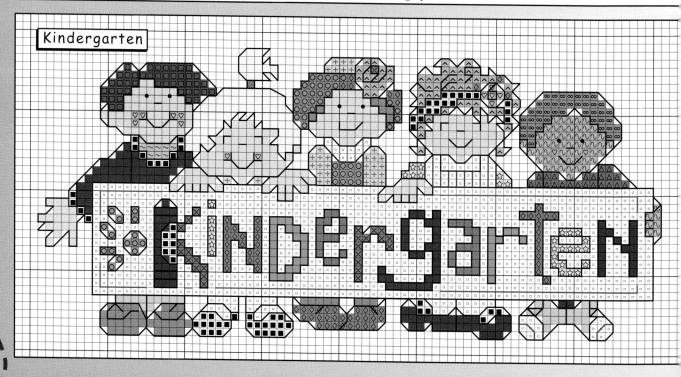

Anchor	DMC
2	blanc
387	712
73	963
75	962
928	3761
168	807
1008	3773
1007	3772
234	762
403	310

Backstitch:

76/961—white cat's nose, mouth, chin wrinkle

169/806—paw print

1007—cream cat (except eyes, nose, mouth, chin wrinkle)

400/317—bow, white cat (except eyes)

403—all eyes, cream cat's nose, mouth, chin wrinkle

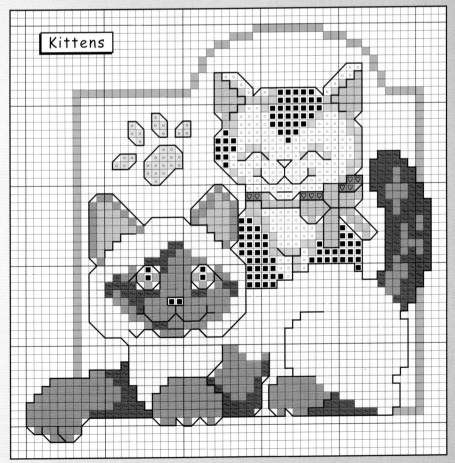

Kittens

K is for...

Kayak

Kilt

Anchor	DMC
334	606
778	3774
302	743
210	562
160	827
109	209
884	356
403	310

Backstitch:
884—skin, hair
400/317—clothes, kayak,
    paddle (except shaft)
403—glasses, paddle shaft

Kayak

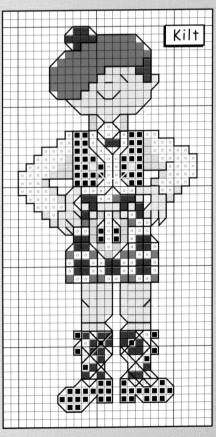

Kilt

Anchor	DMC
2	blanc
334	606
778	3774
306	783
209	913
128	800
884	356
403	310

Backstitch:
(2 strands)—vest chain
884—skin, hair
400/317—hat, shirt
403—eye, remaining clothes,
shoes

K is for...

Anchor	DMC	Anchor	DMC
2	blanc	108	210
24	963	883	3064
334	606	881	945
1006	304	1047	402
323	3825	1082	841
295	726	1086	839
366	951	234	762
368	437	399	318
167	519	403	310
168	807		

French Knots: 403
Backstitch:
110/208—kite tail
351/400—kite bear (except face),
    kiss bear (except face)
1086—koala (except face)
400/317—kite, kite string, kite
    bear's shirt, koala's bow, kiss
    bear's bow, cat (except face)
403—kite bear's face, koala's face,
    kiss bear's face, cat's face

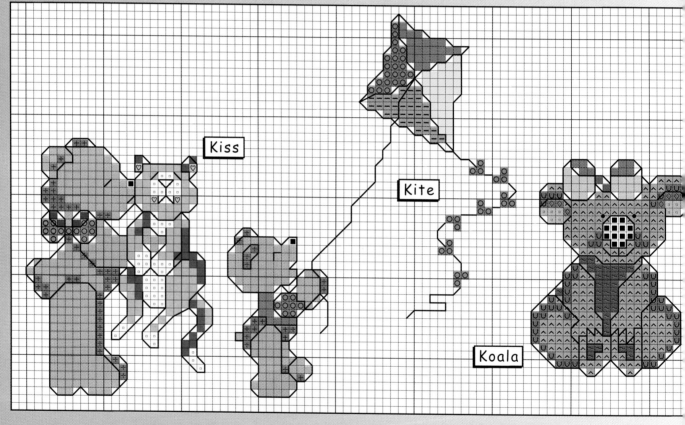

Kiss   Kite   Koala

Love
Longhorn
Lollipops
Lipstick
Light
Lightbulbs
Leash

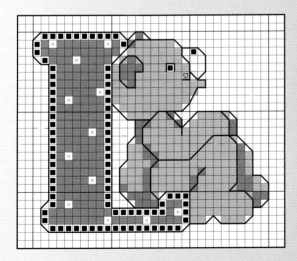

Anchor	DMC
2	blanc
387	712
24	963
109	209
881	945
1047	402
403	310

Backstitch:
351/400—bear (except eye, nose, mouth)
403—eye, nose, mouth, "L"

Anchor	DMC	Backstitch:
2	blanc	1005—flower
387	712	210/562—leaves
334	606	351/400—bears (except
1005	816	eyes, noses, mouths)
314	741	400/317—balloon, red
305	743	hearts, bows
209	913	403—remaining outlines
881	945	
1047	402	
403	310	

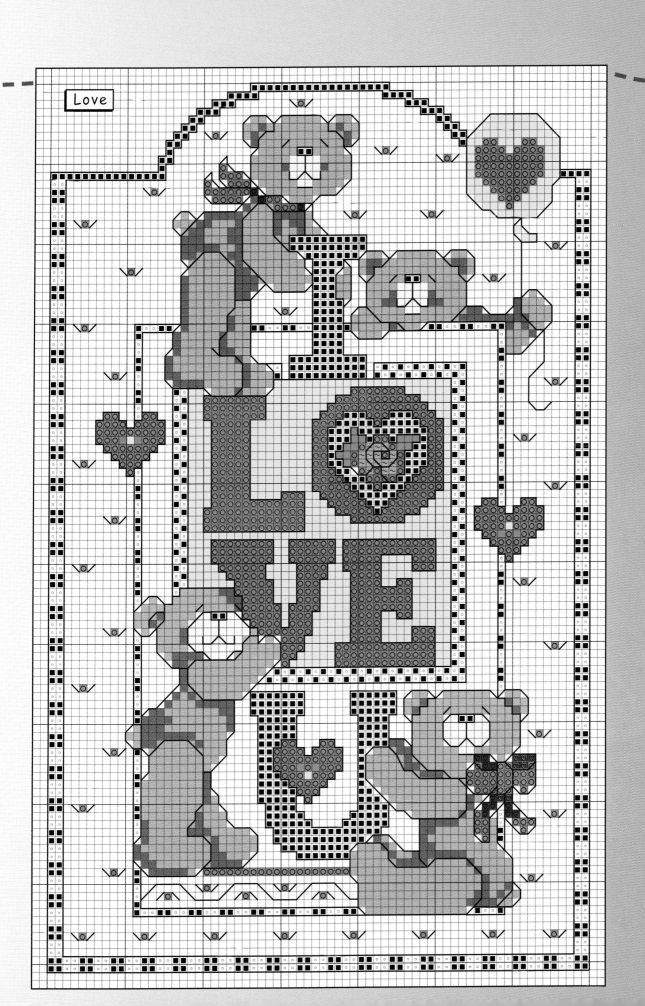

Love

L is for... Longhorn

Anchor	DMC
2	blanc
885	739
24	963
347	402
349	301
234	762
399	318

French Knots: 403/310
Backstitch:
349—steer (except horns,
    mouth, hoofs)
400/317—horns, hooves
403—mouth

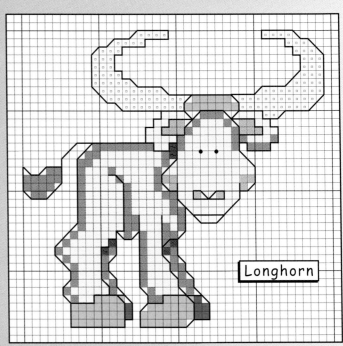

Longhorn

Lollipops

Anchor	DMC	French Knots:
2	blanc	87—second "LOLLIPOP"
366	951	226—first "LOLLIPOP"
334	606	**Backstitch:**
87	3607	334—heart
329	3340	87—first lollipop spiral, second
305	743	"lollipop"
226	703	226—second lollipop leaves, fourth
130	809	lollipop spiral, first "lollipop"
97	554	349/301—sticks, flower
		400/317—bows, lollipop outlines

Lipstick

Light

Lightbulbs

YOU LIGHT UP MY LIFE

Anchor	DMC		Anchor	DMC
2	blanc		301	744
1094	605		305	726
333	608		302	743
334	606		254	3348
96	3609		161	813
778	3774		342	211
303	742		109	209
329	3340		403	310
300	745		701 (muliné lamé)	

French Knots:
168/807—"YOU," "UP MY LIFE"
701—"LIGHT"

Backstitch:
57/602—cheeks
333—nose, lips, lipstick (except case)
306/783—light rays on single bulb
168—"YOU," "UP MY LIFE"
883/3064—light glow on multiple bulbs
884/356—all bulbs, single bulb base, hair, skin
403—eyes, clothes, lipstick case, hair tie
701—multiple bulb bases, "LIGHT"

L is for...

Leash

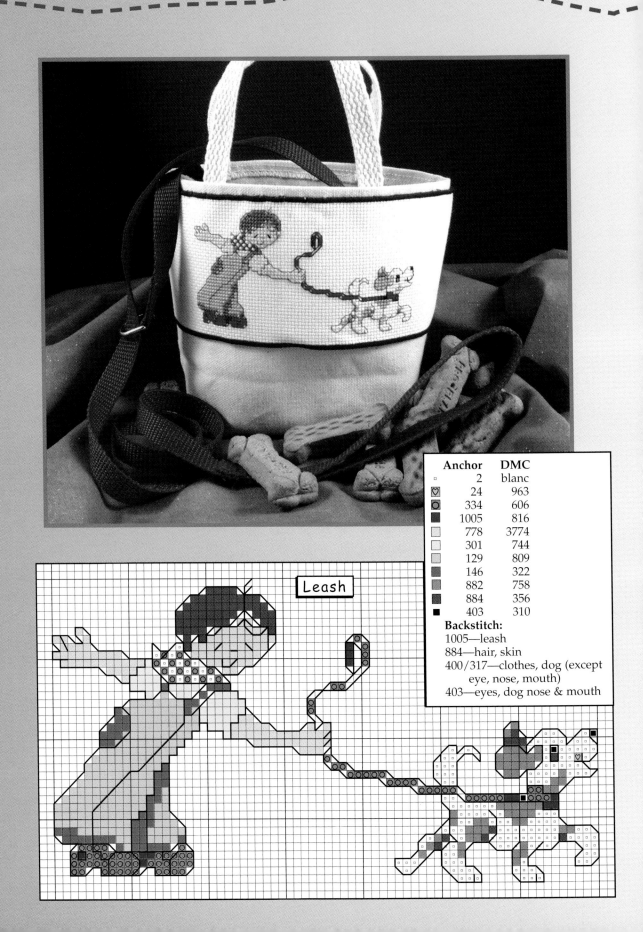

Anchor	DMC
2	blanc
24	963
334	606
1005	816
778	3774
301	744
129	809
146	322
882	758
884	356
403	310

Backstitch:
1005—leash
884—hair, skin
400/317—clothes, dog (except
eye, nose, mouth)
403—eyes, dog nose & mouth

Leash

M is for...

Moon
Mask
Music
Monk
Mom
Magnify
Mouse
Milk
March
Monkeys
Magic

Anchor	DMC
2	blanc
387	712
334	606
293	727
96	3609
881	945
1047	402
403	310

Backstitch:
351/400—bear (except eyes,
   nose, mouth)
400/317—clothes
403—eyes, nose, mouth, "M"

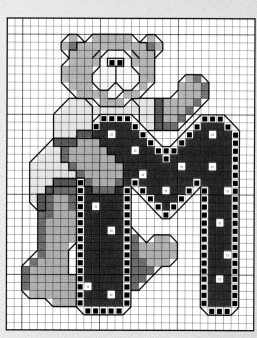

M is for...

Moon

Mask

Music

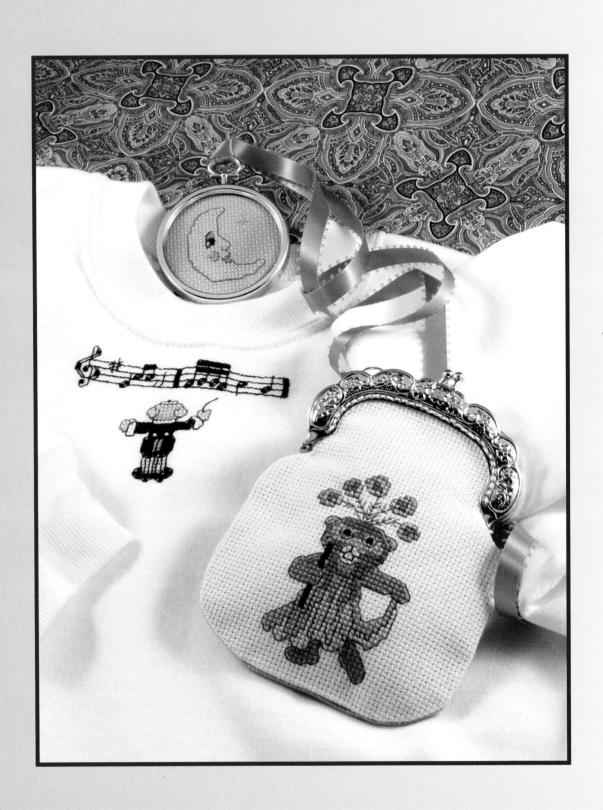

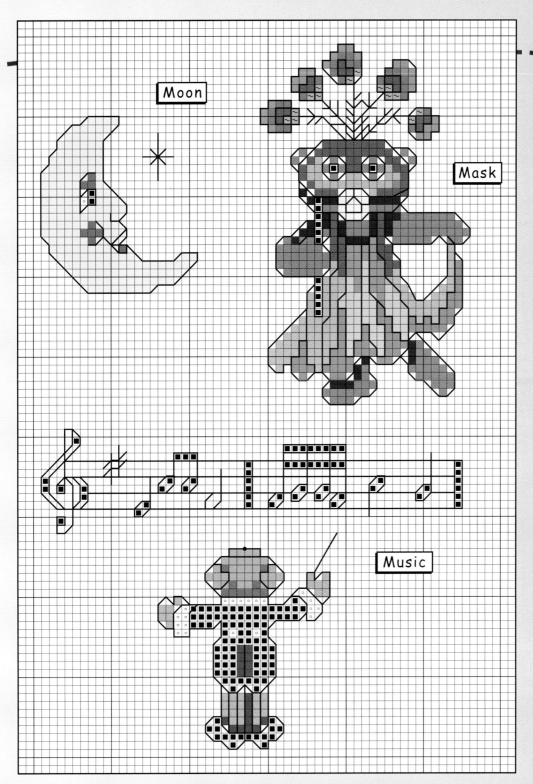

Anchor	DMC	Anchor	DMC
2	blanc	98	553
387	712	883	3064
301	744	1007	3772
206	564	881	945
928	3811	1047	402
167	519	234	762
168	3810	399	318
96	3609	403	310

French Knot: 403
Eyelet: 701 (muliné lamé)
Backstitch:
169/806—feathers (except centers)
351/400—bears (except eyes)
1049/3826—moon (except eye)
400/317—mask (except handle),
   dress, feather centers
403—moon's eye, music, music bear's
   clothes, baton, mask handle,
   mask bear's eyes & mouth

M is for...

Monk

Mom

Anchor	DMC		Anchor	DMC
2	blanc		1092	964
885	739		186	959
24	963		120	3747
334	606		96	3609
778	3774		347	402
868	758		390	3033
301	744		1082	841
302	743		1084	840
361	738		400	317
206	564		403	310

French Knots: 403

Backstitch:

39/309—monk's, mom's & baby's mouths

334—diaper bag stripes

187/958—mom's shirt sleeve stripes

884/356—rabbit (except nose); monk's, mom's & baby's skin; mom's & baby's hair

1086/839—monk's hair, robe, sandals

400—lamb; mom's clothes & shoes; baby's clothes, shoes & bow; stroller; remaining diaper bag; pin; bottle; box

403—monk's eyes; rabbit's nose; lamb's nose, mouth, hooves & ears

Anchor	DMC
2	blanc
387	712
24	963
39	309
334	606
323	3825
301	744
302	743
311	3827
842	3013
843	3012
185	964
128	800
881	945
1047	402
1049	301
234	762
399	318
400	317
403	310

French Knots:
400—mouse's nose
403—ant's eye & antennae

Backstitch:
39—cat's tongue
334—"MILK"
136/799—magnifying
     glass lines
1049—cheese
884/356—cat
351/400—bear (except eye,
     nose, mouth)
400—bottle, milk, mouse,
     hat, clothes, magnifying
     glass
403—ant, bear's eye, nose
     & mouth

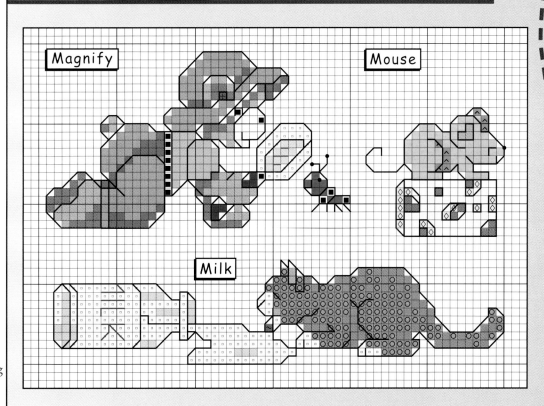

M is for...

Anchor	DMC
2	blanc
24	963
334	606
302	743
361	738
136	799
881	945
1080	842
1084	840
235	414
403	310

French Knots: 403
Backstitch:
334—monkeys' mouths
349/301—rabbit
351/400—bear (except eyes, nose)
1086/839—monkeys (except eyes, muzzles)
403—monkeys' eyes & muzzles; bear's eyes, nose, wand, clothes; rabbit's hat & wand

March

Monkeys

Magic

Ñ is for...

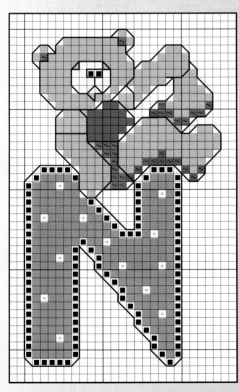

Anchor	DMC
2	blanc
387	712
329	3340
160	827
161	813
881	945
1047	405
403	310

Backstitch:
351/400—bear (except
  eyes, nose)
400/317—shirt
403—eyes, nose, "N"

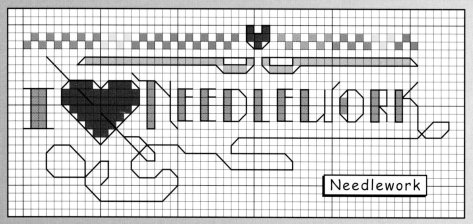

Anchor	DMC
334	606
97	554
329	3340
305	743
225	703
1039	518
108	210
234	762

Backstitch:
334—large heart
111/208—lettering, thread
400/317—needles
403/310—small heart

Needlework

Anchor	DMC	Anchor	DMC
2	blanc	928	3761
387	712	168	807
1021	761	129	809
1023	3712	136	799
778	3774	1080	842
10	351	234	762
1025	347	399	318
347	402	403	310

French Knots: 403
Backstitch:
1024/3328—dog's tongue
39/309—boy's mouth
162/517—"NEWFY"
884/356—bag, boy's hair & skin
400/317—shirt, pants, shoes
403—dog, paw prints, papers,
    belt, laces, "NEWS"

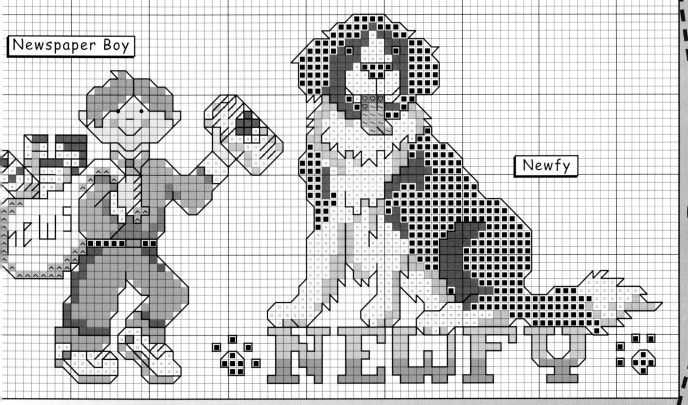

Newspaper Boy

Newfy

NEWFY

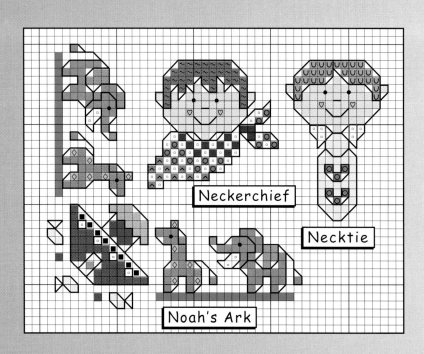

Anchor	DMC
2	blanc
24	963
334	606
46	666
1005	816
778	3774
323	722
329	3340
295	726
311	676
210	562
159	3325
146	322
884	356
1048	3776
1082	841
234	762
403	310

French Knots: 403
Backstitch:
146—collar stripes
884—neckerchief boy's hair,
 giraffes, boys' skin,
 fish, ark
1086/839—necktie boy's hair
400/317—neckerchief,
 remaining shirt, necktie,
 elephants

Neckerchief

Necktie

Noah's Ark

O is for...

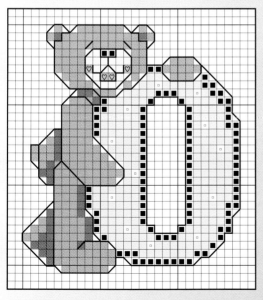

Anchor	DMC
2	blanc
387	712
24	963
305	743
881	945
1047	402
403	310

Backstitch:
351/400—bear (except eyes,
    nose, mouth)
403—eyes, nose, mouth, "O"

Anchor	DMC		Anchor	DMC		Anchor	DMC		Anchor	DMC
2	blanc		885	739		366	951		351	400
933	543		305	743		378	841		831	3782
36	3326		361	738		936	632		832	612
882	758		891	676		358	433		905	3021
884	356		120	3747		360	898		399	318
323	722		159	3325		881	945		403	310
314	741		161	813		1047	402			
324	721		95	554		1048	3776			
326	720		97	553		1049	301			

French Knot: 403
Straight Stitch (otter's whiskers): 403
Backstitch:
162/825—opossum's bow, otter's water
936—owl (except eyes, beak)
1049—owl's beak

351—ostrich's beak & legs, bear (except nose, mouth)
905—bear's boots
400/317—remaining ostrich (except eye), opossum (except eye, mouth)

403—ostrich's eye, otter, otter's ball, oriole, owl's eyes, bear's nose & mouth, opossum's eye & mouth

Owl

Oriole

Opossum

Otter

Ostrich

Overshoes

O is for...

Anchor	DMC
2	blanc
24	963
334	606
46	666
778	3774
868	758
301	744
241	966
244	987
159	3325
161	813
403	310

French Knots: 403

Backstitch:
5975/356—bandage
161—overall bib stripes
884/920—boy's skin & hair
400/317—boy's clothes,
    shoes, lettering
403—exclamation point

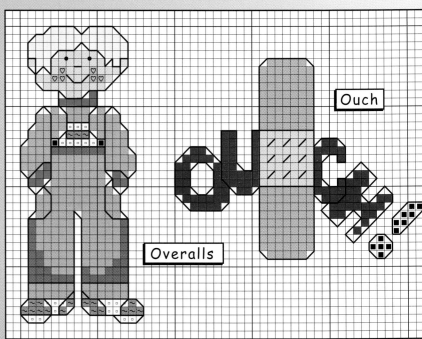

Ouch

Overalls

P is for...

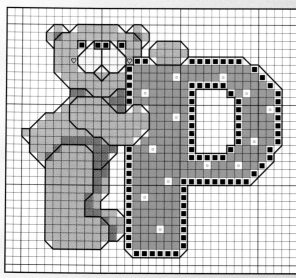

Anchor	DMC
2	blanc
387	712
36	3326
241	966
881	945
1047	402
403	310

Backstitch:
351/400—bear (except eyes, nose, mouth)
403—eyes, nose, mouth, "P"

P is for...

Puppy Love

Pawprint

Puppy Litter

Anchor	DMC
2	blanc
36	3326
39	309
334	606
1006	304
882	758
884	356
314	741
305	743
361	738
363	436
241	966
129	809
96	3609
347	402
398	415
235	414
403	310

French Knots:
39—paw prints
403—eyes

Backstitch:
39—basset's tongue, black dog's tongue, "PUPPY LOVE"
169/806—bee wing
349/301—puppy litter (except noses & mouths)
936/632—basset (except nose & mouth), retriever (except nose & muzzle)
400/317—white dog (except nose), paw print, bow
403—remaining bee, black dog, all noses & mouths, retriever muzzle

Puppy Love

Pawprint

Puppy Litter

PUPPY LOVE

Anchor	DMC		Anchor	DMC		Anchor	DMC
2	blanc		187	958		914	407
367	738		161	813		403	310
23	3713		128	775			
25	3326		1090	996			
76	3731		1089	995			
50	3716		130	809			
38	961		178	791			
97	554		108	210			
329	3340		109	209			
185	964		119	333			

Backstitch:
42/326—pink ice cream, pig (except eyes & mouth)
1007/3772—brown ice cream, cone, penguin's beak
& feet
400/317—remaining penguin (except eye), pig's
bow, bear (except eye, nose, mouth)
403—penguin's eye; pig's eyes & mouth; bear's
eye, nose, mouth

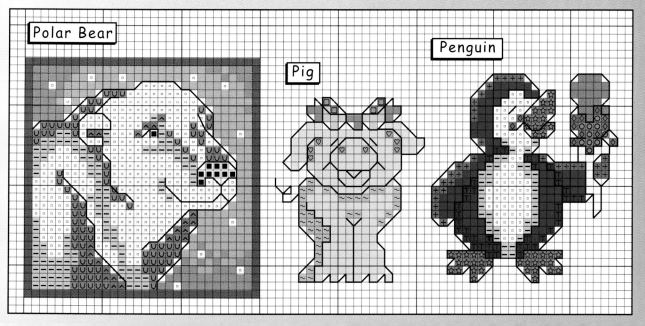

Polar Bear

Pig

Penguin

P is for... Panda

Anchor	DMC	Anchor	DMC
2	blanc	234	762
276	739	235	414
36	3326	403	310
259	772	701 (muliné lamé)	
238	703	**Backstitch:**	
244	987	217/561—leaves, stems	
347	402	884—bamboo	
884	356	403—bears	

Panda

P is for...

Paint   Pajamas

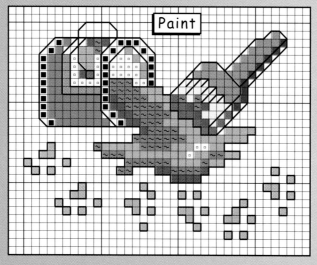

Anchor	DMC
◦ 2	blanc
□ 366	951
46	666
■ 1005	816
242	989
96	3609
≈ 100	552
102	550
347	402
234	762
■ 403	310

Backstitch:
100—paw prints
102—paint
1007/3772—brush bristles
400/317—can handle, brush handle
403—can

118

Pajamas

Anchor	DMC
2	blanc
24	963
26	894
28	892
778	3774
891	676
901	680
398	415
235	414
403	310

French Knots: 403

Backstitch:

28—mouth, pajama flap
   buttonhole

897/221—remaining
   pajamas

1007/3772—skin

400/317—bear (except
   eyes)

403—bear's eyes

308—hair

P is for...

Parachute

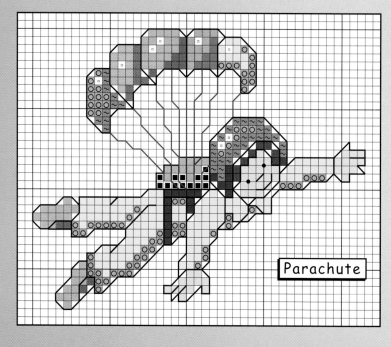

	Anchor	DMC
▫	2	blanc
~	334	606
◼	1006	304
☐	778	3774
◎	303	742
	305	743
	241	966
	244	987
	129	809
	146	322
	108	210
	110	208
	936	632
	235	414
◼	403	310

French Knots: 403
Backstitch:
334—parachute cords
1007/3772—skin
936—hair
400/317—remaining
outlines

Parachute

Q is for...

Anchor	DMC
2	blanc
387	712
209	913
103	3609
96	3608
881	945
1047	402
403	310

Backstitch:
351/400—bear (except eyes, nose)
400/317—shirt
403—eyes, nose, "Q"

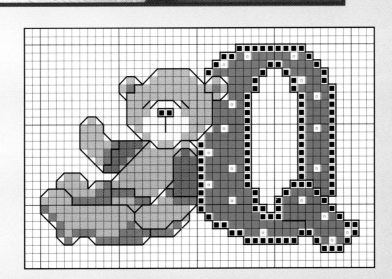

Anchor	DMC
⸳ 2	blanc
☐ 361	738
∧ 24	963
306	783
109	209
881	945
1003	922
■ 403	310

French Knot: 403
Backstitch:
351/400—crown, cats
   (except eyes,
   noses, mouth)
400/317—robe
403—eyes, noses,
   mouth

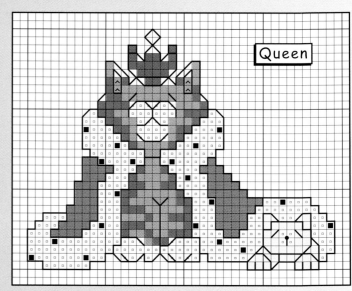

Queen

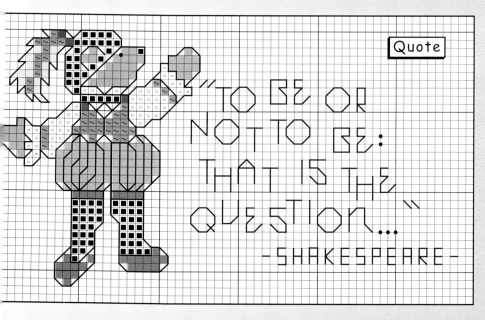

Anchor	DMC
2	blanc
334	606
1006	304
302	743
96	3609
98	553
881	945
403	310

Quote

French Knots:
146/322—lettering
403—eye

Backstitch:
1005/816—feather
146—"TO . . . QUESTION"
111/208—pants, "
  -SHAKESPEARE-"
351/400—bear (except
  nose)
400/317—shirt, shoes
403—hat, nose, tie, vest,
  stockings

Q is for...

Question Mark

Quill

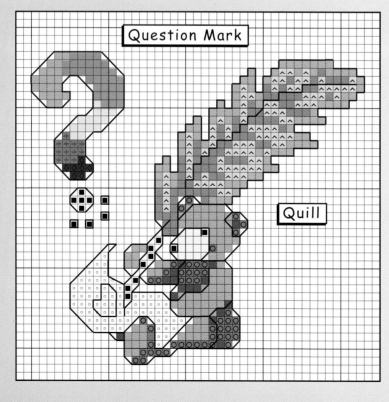

Question Mark

Quill

	Anchor	DMC
▫	2	blanc
☐	387	712
◈	334	606
∧	103	3609
▨	96	3608
⊞	329	3340
☐	305	743
▨	241	966
▨	130	809
▨	108	210
▨	881	945
◉	1047	402
▨	1049	301
■	403	310

Backstitch:
334—heart
110/208—feather
351/400—bear (except
  eye, nose)
400/317—paper, question
  mark (except paw
  print)
403—pen, nose, eye,
  paw print

124

Anchor	DMC
2	blanc
334	606
96	3609
314	741
305	743
241	966
161	813
136	799
109	209
882	758
1007	3772
403	310

French Knots: 403
Backstitch:
334—lettering, strings
110/208—line under ducks
349/301—small ducks, large
  duck's beak
400/317—small ducks' wheels
403—remaining large duck,
  large duck's wheel, quails

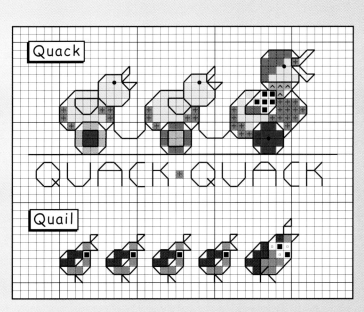

Q is for...   Quiet

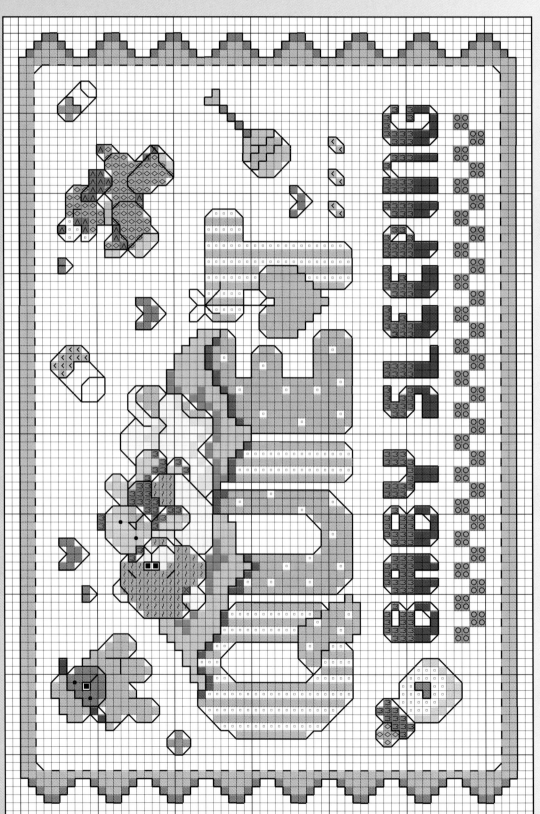

Anchor	DMC		Anchor	DMC
2	blanc		1043	369
885	739		241	966
74	3354		185	964
38	961		1031	3753
8	353		129	809
9	352		146	322
10	351		108	210
323	722		347	402
324	721		349	301
201	3348		403	310

French Knots: 403

Backstitch:

39/309—border, heart on string, heart on bottle
211/562—blanket
1076/991—turquoise pin, dots following "QUIET"
147/797—blue teddy (except nose), heart string, bottle (except nipple), "BABY SLEEPING"
351/400—brown bear (except eyes, nose, mouth), yellow pajamas, bottle nipple
400/317—lamb (except nose), remaining hearts, dog, purple pin, rattle, purple dot, "QUIET"
403—lamb's nose; brown bear's eyes, nose, mouth; blue bear's nose

Q is for... Quilt

Anchor	DMC
2	blanc
387	712
328	3341
301	744
302	743
361	738
1043	369
241	966
185	964
168	807
1031	3753
129	809
136	799
95	554
881	945
1047	402
1049	301
403	310

Backstitch:
137/798—apron stripes
110/208—thread
351/400—bear (except eyes, nose, mouth), chair, hoop
400/317—clothes, quilt, glasses
403—eyes, nose, mouth, needle

Quilt

R is for...

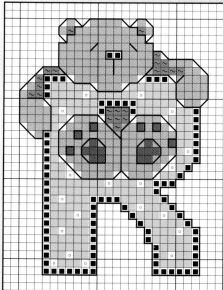

Anchor	DMC
2	blanc
186	959
881	945
1047	402
1049	301
403	310

Backstitch:
351/400—bear (except eyes, nose)
403—eyes, nose, "R"

R is for...

Rhinoceros

Raccoon

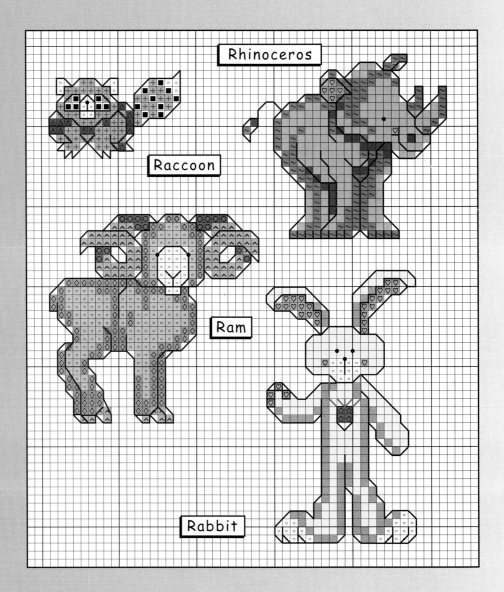

Anchor	DMC	French Knots:
2	blanc	401/413—rhino eye
387	712	403/310—rabbit eyes, rac-
24	963	coon nose, ram eyes
323	722	**Backstitch:**
885	739	210/562—necklace, carrot top
361	738	1007/3772—rabbit (except
367	437	nose), carrot
391	303	393/640—ram (except nose)
392	642	1086/839—raccoon (except
390	3033	eyes, ears, nose, tail)
899	3782	401—rhino
397	3042	403—rabbit nose; ram nose;
399	318	raccoon eyes, ears, nose,
235	414	& tail
400	317	

R is for...

Rainbow

Roast Marshmallows

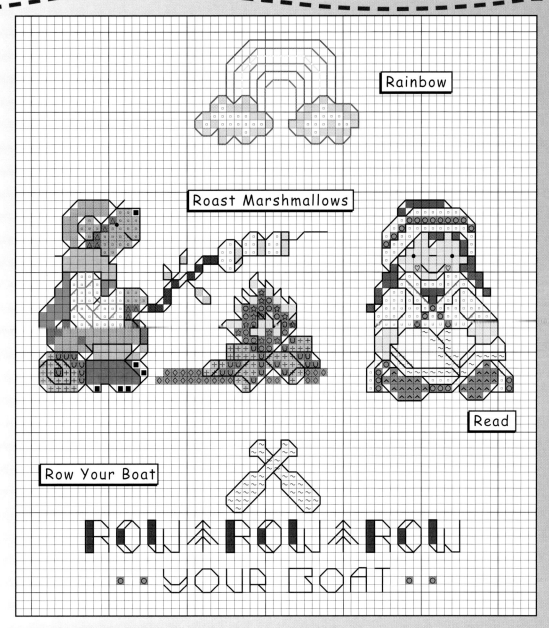

Rainbow

Roast Marshmallows

Read

Row Your Boat

Anchor	DMC		Anchor	DMC
2	blanc		128	775
387	712		129	809
367	738		146	322
24	963		1080	842
334	606		378	841
43	814		1007	3772
778	3774		881	945
329	3340		1047	402
305	743		884	356
886	677		1086	839
874	834		233	451
241	966		235	414
877	502		403	310

French Knots: 403
Backstitch:
39/309—girl's mouth
334—first rainbow stripe
43—"ROW ROW ROW"
329—second rainbow stripe
—third rainbow stripe
226/703—fourth rainbow
    stripe
244—leaves on stick
217/561—pine trees, "YOUR
    BOAT"
878/501—bear's shirt sleeve
    pattern

146—fifth rainbow stripe,
    clouds, girl's collar &
    sleeve stripes
97/554—sixth rainbow
    stripe
1007—oars, bear (except
    nose), stick, logs, fire,
    girl's skin
884—girl's hair
400/317—bear's clothes &
    hat, marshmallows,
    girl's clothes & hat,
    book
403—bear's nose & boots

Anchor	DMC
2	blanc
48	3689
50	3716
27	899
29	309
334	606
95	554
97	553
323	722
302	743
241	966
209	913
136	799
108	210
110	208
234	762
403	310

French Knot: 1005/816
Backstitch:
42/326—pig (except eye)
1005—"ARE WE THERE YET?"
403—pig's eye, tires
400/317—remaining outlines

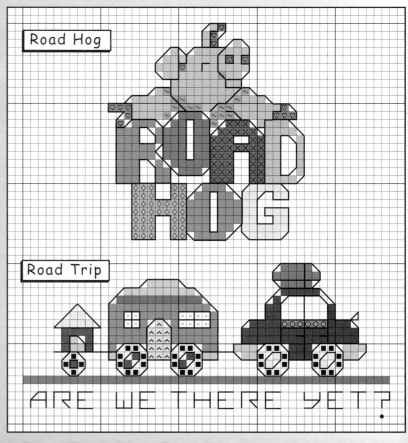

Road Hog

Road Trip

ARE WE THERE YET?

"S is for...

Scarecrow
Snowman
Sunglasses
Seal
Snorkel
Seahorse
Socks
Slippers
Shoes
Skateboard

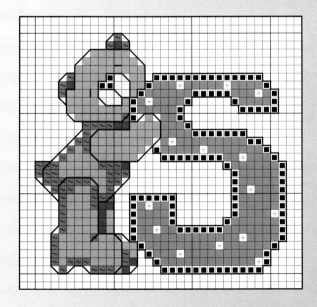

Anchor	DMC
2	blanc
387	712
136	799
881	945
1047	402
1049	301
403	310

Backstitch:
351/400—bear (except eyes, nose, mouth)
403—eyes, nose, mouth, "S"

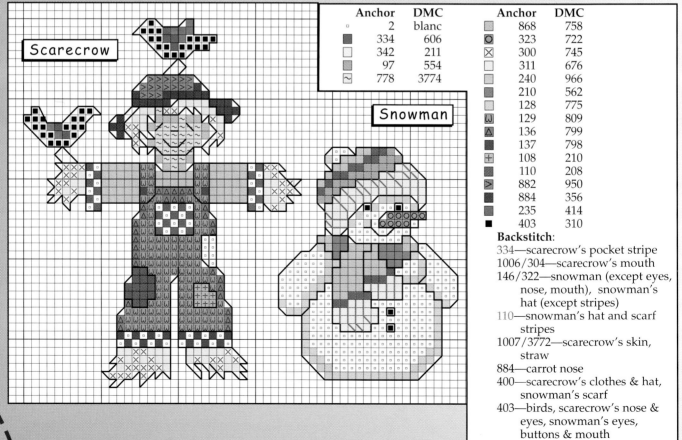

Anchor	DMC
2	blanc
334	606
342	211
97	554
778	3774

	Anchor	DMC
	868	758
◉	323	722
⊠	300	745
	311	676
	240	966
	210	562
	128	775
ш	129	809
△	136	799
	137	798
＋	108	210
	110	208
▷	882	950
	884	356
	235	414
■	403	310

Backstitch:
334—scarecrow's pocket stripe
1006/304—scarecrow's mouth
146/322—snowman (except eyes, nose, mouth), snowman's hat (except stripes)
110—snowman's hat and scarf stripes
1007/3772—scarecrow's skin, straw
884—carrot nose
400—scarecrow's clothes & hat, snowman's scarf
403—birds, scarecrow's nose & eyes, snowman's eyes, buttons & mouth

Sunglasses   Seal   Snorkel   Seahorse

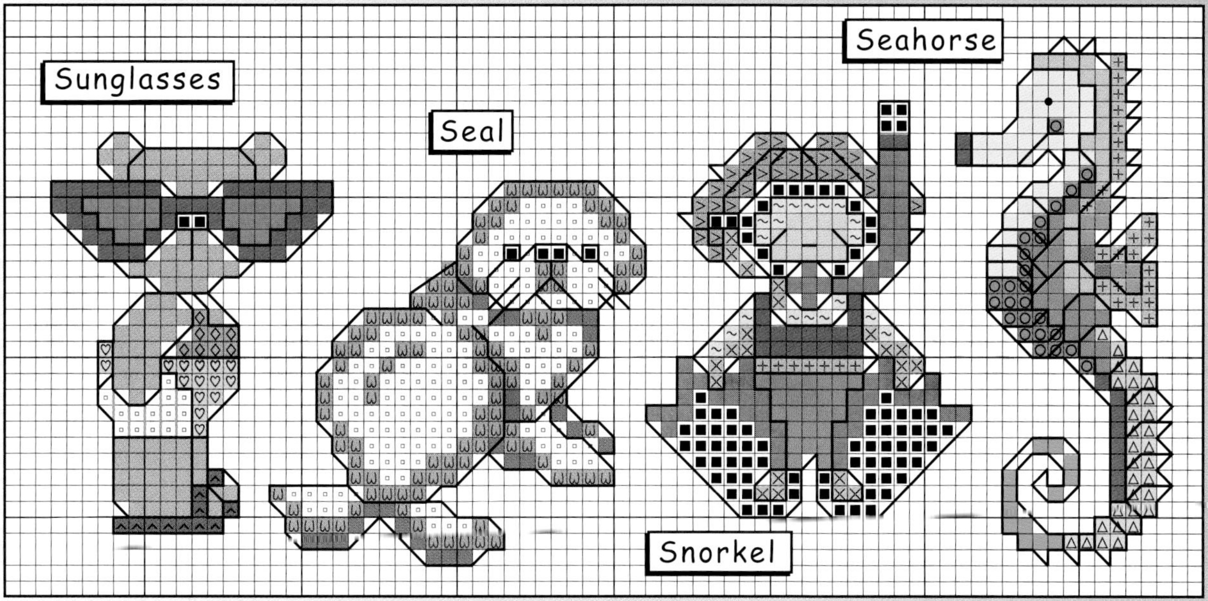

	Anchor	DMC		Anchor	DMC
▫	2	blanc	Δ	928	3761
	334	606		168	807
♡	96	3609		128	775
	97	554	ω	120	3747
~	778	3774		121	809
×	868	758	+	108	210
O	330	947		110	208
	302	743		881	945
>	311	676	^	884	356
◇	253	472		235	414
	1043	369	■	403	310
	241	966			

French Knot: 403

Backstitch:

97—bear's short stripes

169/806—seahorse (except nose & mouth)

1007/3772—snorkeler's skin, hair

884—bear (except nose), bear's sandals

400/317—sunglasses, bear's remaining clothes, seal (except eyes, nose, whiskers)

403—bear's nose; seal's eyes, nose, whiskers, snorkeler's gear, clothes; seahorse's nose & mouth

Anchor	DMC
2	blanc
73	963
75	962
76	961
334	606
103	3609
96	3608
329	3340
314	711
301	744
1043	369
206	564
1092	959
168	807
128	775
129	809
146	322
109	209
111	208
400	317
403	310

French Knots: 403

Backstitch:

65/3085—bunny slippers
(except mouths)

169/806—lettering

146—bear slippers
(except noses,
mouths), blue shoe
(except flower)

349/301—blue shoe
flower

400—turquoise shoe, red
shoe (except laces &
heel), hearts

403—bunny slipper
mouths, bear slipper
noses & mouths,
panda, socks, red
shoe laces & heel

Skateboard

Anchor	DMC
47	321
778	3774
868	758
305	743
306	783
254	3348
136	799
97	554
884	356
403	310

Backstitch:
1006/304—mouth
884—skin, hair
400/317—clothes
 (except belt),
 shoes, skateboard
403—belt, eyes

T is for...

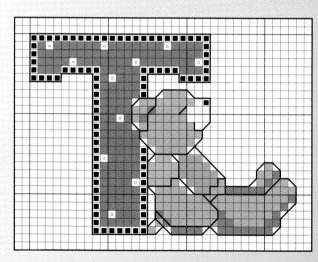

Anchor	DMC
2	blanc
387	712
206	564
129	809
86	3608
881	945
1047	402
403	310

Backstitch:
351/400—bear (except eye, nose)
400/317—shirt
403—eye, nose, "T"

Anchor	DMC
2	blanc
24	963
334	606
778	3774
868	758
301	744
302	743
875	503
877	502
146	322
1007	3772
403	310

French Knots:
334—exclamation point
403—eyes

Eyelets (stars): 701
(muliné lamé)

Backstitch:
42/326—nose, mouth
334—exclamation point
878/501—tent
147—lettering
1007—tent stakes, feet
884/356—remaining star
400—cap

Twinkle Little Star

Tent

Toothbrush

Tooth

Anchor	DMC
2	blanc
24	963
334	606
778	3774
868	758
882	960
884	356

French Knots:
137/798—lettering
403/310—eyes

Backstitch:
39/309—mouths, toothbrush handle
334—pajama stripes
168/807—toothpaste
137/798—lettering
884—skin
936/632—hair
400/317—toothbrush bristles, remaining pajamas
401/413—remaining tooth

143

Tea Time

Anchor	DMC		Anchor	DMC
2	blanc		145	809
387	712		146	322
24	963		148	312
1006	304		882	758
334	606		883	3064
778	3774		884	920
868	758		881	945
311	676		1047	402
292	3078		234	762
301	744		399	318
305	743		235	414
240	966		403	310
159	3325			

Backstitch:
334—stool stripes
1006/304—hearts, girl's mouth
211/562—leaves
148—decorations on cups,
   teapot, & sugar bowl;
   collar stripes, "TIME"
884—"TEA," steam, roses, skin
351/400—girl's hair, tea bags
   (except tags, staples,
   strings), dog (except eye,
   nose, muzzle), chair

400/317—remaining clothes,
   shoes, cat (except eye),
   remaining stool, kerchiefs,
   tea bag tags, remaining
   cups, teapot, sugar bowl,
   blue lines
403—eyes, dog's nose &
   muzzle, tea bag strings
   & staples

T is for...   Television   Telephone

Anchor	DMC		Anchor	DMC	
▫	2	blanc		875	503
☐	778	3774		877	501
♡	24	963		159	3325
～	334	606		161	813
	1006	304		234	762
○	323	722		235	414
	361	738	■	403	310
	363	436			

French Knot: 403
Backstitch:
884/356—dog (except nose, muzzle)
1007/3772—cat (except eyes, nose)
400/317—television (except knobs), bow
403—eyes, noses, muzzle, television knobs, telephone

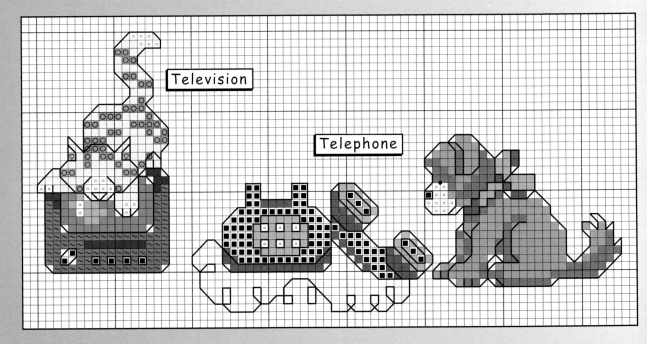

Television

Telephone

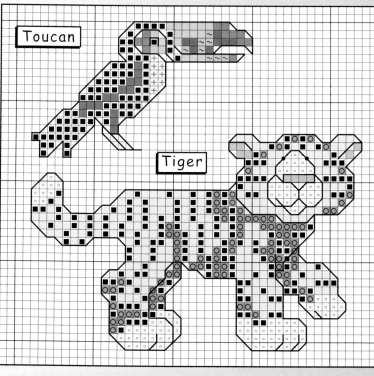

Toucan

Tiger

Anchor	DMC
2	blanc
24	963
334	606
324	721
305	743
311	676
254	3348
226	703
1090	996
137	798
96	3609
235	414
403	310

French Knots: 403
Backstitch:
351/400—tiger (except
nose, mouth, paws,
white tail tip)
403—toucan, tiger's nose,
mouth,
paws, white tail tip

Anchor	DMC
2	blanc
387	712
48	3689
50	3716
38	961
334	606
128	775
129	800
145	809
146	322
881	945
1047	402
1049	301
235	414
403	310

French Knots: 403
Backstitch:
38—dress heart
146—tiara
351/400—bears (except eyes, noses, mouth)
400/317—dress, vest, bowtie
403—eyes, noses, mouth, hat

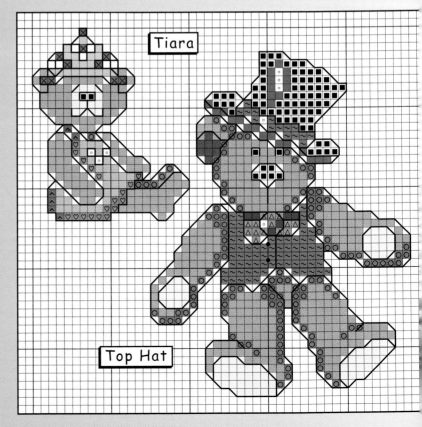

Tiara

Top Hat

U is for...

Anchor	DMC
2	blanc
387	712
1043	369
241	966
109	209
881	945
1047	402
403	310

Backstitch:
351/400—bear (except eye, nose, mouth)
400/317—shirt
403—eye, nose, mouth, "U"

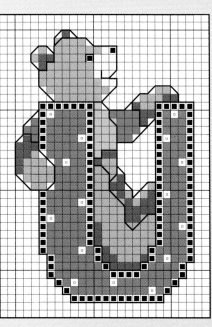

Anchor	DMC
2	blanc
334	606
778	3774
329	3340
311	676
305	743
241	966
1031	3753
129	809
109	209
403	310

French Knots: 403

Backstitch:
146/322—water drops
884/356—hair, skin
400/317—umbrellas (except
   handles, shafts, tips),
   clothes, shoes
403—handles, shafts, tips

Umbrella

Umbrellas

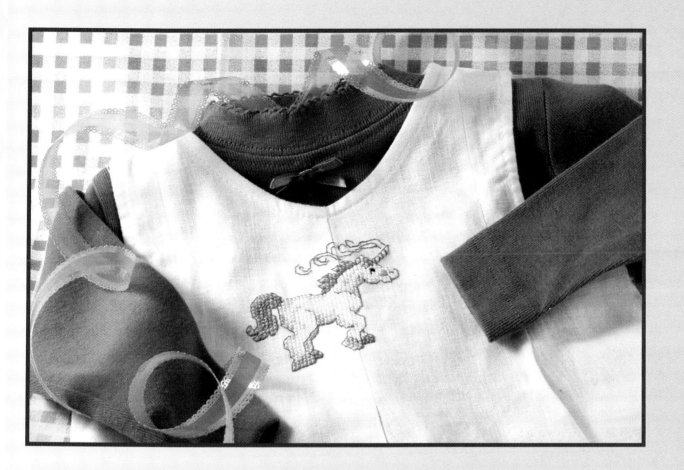

Anchor	DM
2	blanc
26	894
85	3609
97	554
128	775
129	809
136	799
403	310

Backstitch:
87/3607—swirls
142/798—swirls
100/552—swirls,
   horn stripes
922/930—unicorn
   (except eye)
403—eye

U is for...

Us

Upside Down

I Love "U"

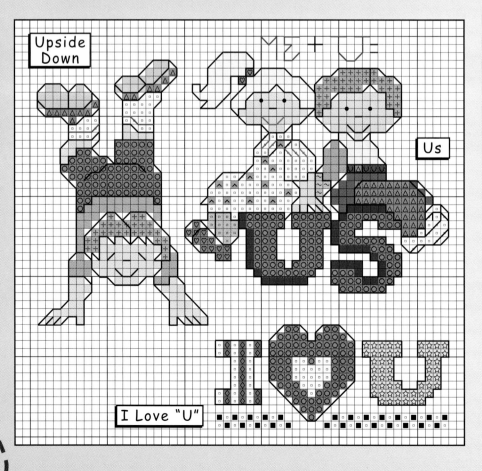

Upside Down

ME + U =

Us

I Love "U"

Anchor	DMC
2	blanc
24	963
26	894
28	892
334	606
1006	304
778	3774
868	758
316	970
301	744
305	743
241	966
1031	3753
129	809
136	799
108	210
1047	402
1048	3776
403	310

French Knots: 403

Backstitch:

39/309—girl's mouth, dress stripes

334—"ME," "U," upside down boy's sock stripes

1049/301—hair, remaining skin

400/317—remaining clothes, shoes,"US," "I♥U"

403—upside down boy's eyes, "+," "="

V is for...

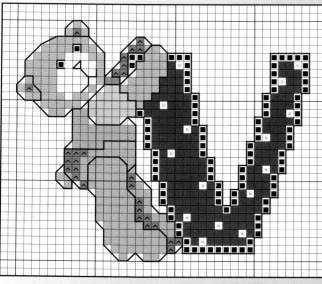

Anchor	DMC
2	blanc
387	712
334	606
240	966
226	703
109	209
881	945
1047	402
403	310

Backstitch:
351/400—bear (except eyes, nose, mouth)
400/317—shirt
403—eyes, nose, mouth, "V"

Anchor	DMC
387	712
24	963
334	606
1005	816
85	3609
97	554
778	3774
868	758
329	3340
305	726
311	676
302	743
842	3013
843	3053
1038	519
920	932
129	809
136	799
109	209
1048	3776
899	3782
903	640
234	762

French Knots: 403/310
Backstitch:
39/309—viking's mouth
884/356—hair, skin
905/3021—sandals
400/317—helmet,
    clothes, shield
401/413—vulture

Anchor	DMC	Backstitch:
▫ 2	blanc	1005—red & yellow vegeta-bles (except stems)
☐ 885	739	211/562—leaves, stems, carrot tops, cauliflower leaves
▨ 24	963	
◮ 334	606	884/356—carrots, rabbit (except eye, nose, muzzle, tail)
■ 1005	816	
◉ 323	722	
☐ 302	743	400/317—cauliflower, wheel barrow (except wheel)
▨ 361	738	
▨ 241	966	403—eye, nose, muzzle, tail, wheel
▨ 210	562	
▨ 129	809	
▨ 235	414	
■ 403	310	

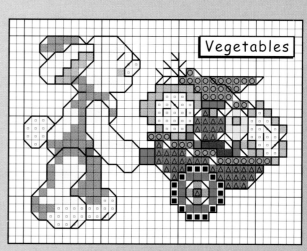

Vegetables

Anchor	DMC	
▫	2	blanc
☐	387	712
⊠	334	606
⊌	1005	816
■	1006	304
▨	96	3609
⊎	11	351
⊙	328	3341
~	301	744
☐	302	743
☐	206	564
◇	204	563
▨	210	562
☐	128	775
△	129	809
▨	146	322
▨	109	209
▨	881	945
▷	1047	402
▨	234	762
▨	399	318
■	403	310

French Knot: 403
Backstitch:
334—bear's skirt
    stripes
1005—roses
146—vase stripes
211/561—leaves,
    stems
351/400—bear (except
    eye, nose, mouth)
400/317—remaining
    vases, clothes, cat,
    vacuum (except
    handle, wheels)
403—eye, nose,
    mouth, handle,
    wheels

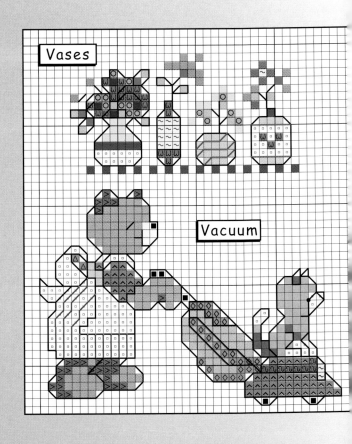

Vases

Vacuum

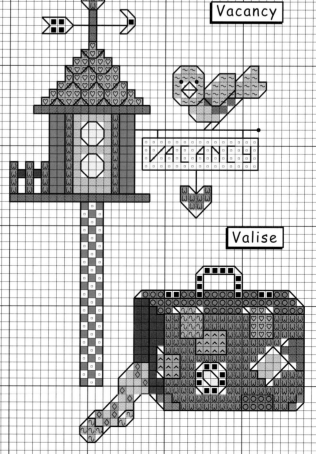

Anchor	DMC
2	blanc
75	962
334	606
1006	304
96	3609
323	722
329	3340
301	744
302	743
1043	369
226	703
205	912
1038	519
160	827
161	813
109	209
403	310

French Knots: 403
Backstitch:
1005/816—"VACANCY"
162/825—bird (except beak, legs)
884/356—beak, legs
400/317—house, fence, sign
401/413—valise (except handle, latches)
403—sign holder, weather-vane, handle, latches

157

Valentine

Anchor	DMC
2	blanc
1020/1021	3713/761
1022	760
206	564
367	738

French Knot: 403/310
Backstitch:
896/3721—hearts
210/562—lettering
884/356—bear (except
    eyes, nose)
403—eyes, nose

Stitching Note: for blended
floss use one strand of each
floss color listed.

Witch
Worry Wart
Wave
Wolf
Whale
Walrus
Wedding
Weathervane
Welcome
Weight

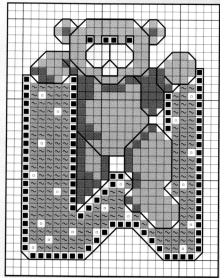

Anchor	DMC
2	blanc
387	712
330	947
881	945
1047	402
403	310

Backstitch:
351/400—bear (except eyes, nose, mouth)
403—eyes, nose, mouth, "W"

159

W is for...

Anchor	DMC
778	3774
300	745
347	402
369	435
351	400
235	414
403	310

French Knot: 403
Backstitch:
42/326—mouth
46/666—broom stripe
351—hair, skin, broom
403—hat, clothes, shoes

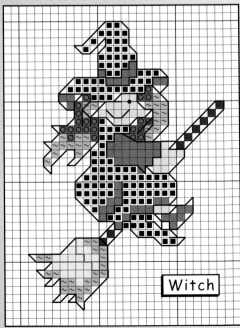

Witch

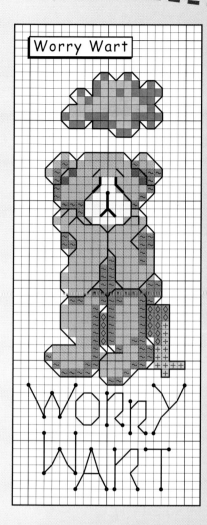

Worry Wart

Anchor	DMC
387	712
881	945
1047	402
1049	301
1082	841
1086	839
234	762
399	318

French Knots:
1005/816—lettering
403/310—nose

Backstitch:
1005—lettering
351/400—bear (except eyes, mouth)
1086—stump
400/317—cloud

Backstitch:
403—(eyes, nose)

W is for...

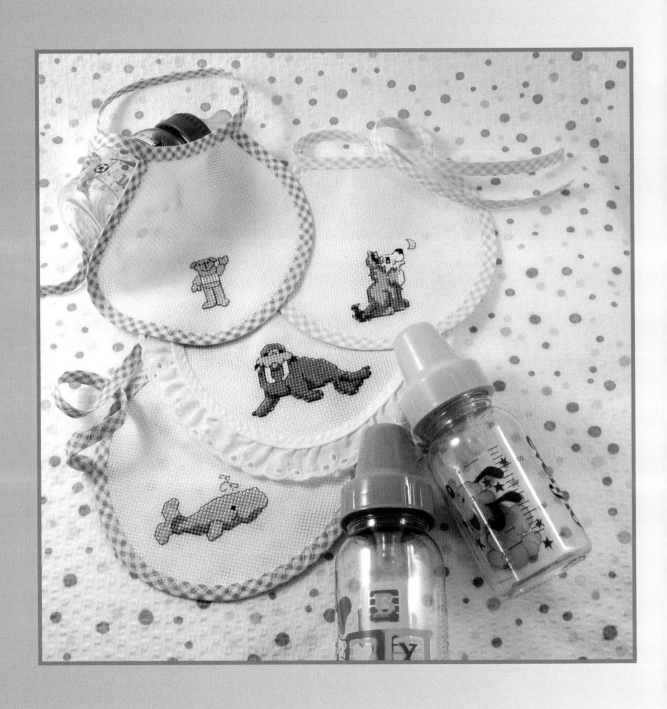

Anchor	DMC		Anchor	DMC
2	blanc		883	3064
24	963		881	945
301	744		378	841
1092	959		936	632
185	964		234	762
120	3747		403	310
121	809			
109/399	209/318			
1030	3746			
367	738			

French Knots: 403
Straight Stitch (walrus'
  whiskers): 403

Backstitch:
187/958—shirt stripes
146/322—water spout
122/3807—whale (except
  eye)
884/356—moon
351/400—bear (except nose)
936—wolf (except nose, eye)
400/317—bear's remaining
  shirt

401/413—walrus (except
  eyes)
403—bear's nose, wolf's
  nose & eye, walrus'
  eyes, whale's eye

Stitching Note: For blended
floss use one strand of each
floss color listed.

Wedding

Anchor	DMC
2	blanc
74	3354
75	962
42	326
778	3774
868	758
301	744
1043	369
204	563
1092	964
186	959
1031	3753
884	356
234	762
235	414

French Knots: 403/310
Backstitch:
42—bride's mouth, groom's tie stripes, heart
210/562—bouquet (except holder), streamers
187/958—gown stripes
146/322—headpiece, veil, remaining gown
884—hair, skin
235—pant stripes, bouquet holder
400/317—groom's remaining clothes, shoes

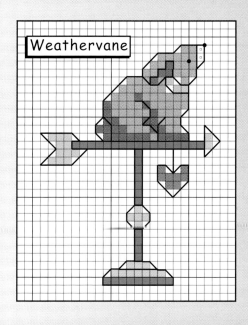

Weathervane

Anchor	DMC
2	blanc
38	961
185	964
217	561
881	945
882	758

French Knots: 403/310
Backstitch:
39/309—heart
217　heart string
400/317—remaining
　outlines

Welcome

	Anchor	DMC		Anchor	DMC
□	2	blanc		1043	369
◹	386	3823	◁	241	966
	334	606		210	562
	1005	816		128	775
	778	3774	~	136	799
	868	758		914	407
◯	323	722		884	356
◑	330	947		234	762
□	301	744	△	235	414
	302	743	◻	403	310
	303	742			

French Knot: 403
Backstitch:
1005—red hat, heart
212/561—eaves, heart ribbons, blond girl's sock stripes
940/792—bee wings, lettering
884—hair, skin, sun, butterfly (except antennae), bee body, rose
403—butterfly & bee antennae, eyelashes, black hat, clothes, shoes, sign border

Anchor	DMC
2	blanc
387	712
73	963
75	962
120	3747
121	809
881	945
1047	402
403	310

Backstitch:
351/400—bear (except eye, nose, mouth)
400/317—towel
403—eye, nose, mouth, scale

Weight

X is for...

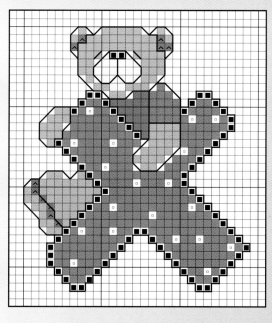

Anchor	DMC
2	blanc
387	712
328	3341
130	809
96	3609
881	945
1047	402
403	310

Backstitch:
351/400—bear (except eyes, nose, mouth)
400/317—shirt
403—eyes, nose, mouth, "X"

X is for...

Anchor	DMC
334	606
1005	816
96	3609
329	3340
305	743
238	703
136	799
881	945
1047	402
403	310

French Knots: 403
Backstitch:
1005—mallets
351/400—bear
   (except face)
400/317—vest
403—face, xylophone

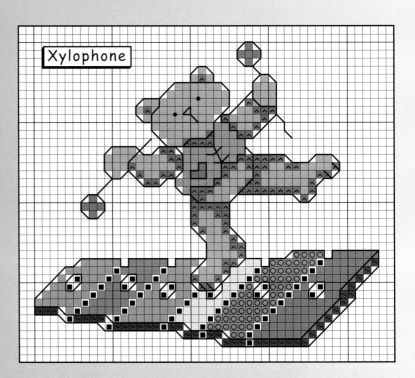

Xylophone

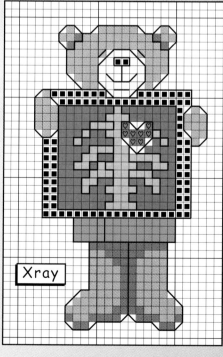

Xray

Anchor	DMC
387	712
334	606
203	564
881	945
1047	402
234	762
235	414
403	310

Backstitch:
1005—heart
351—bear (except eyes, nose, mouth)
400—bones, shorts
403—x-ray, eyes, nose, mouth

X is for...

eXcellent

foXXXy

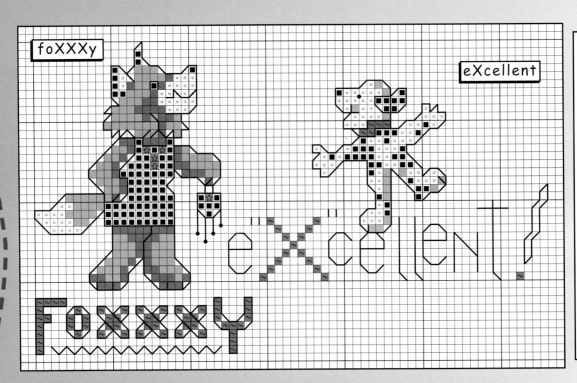

foXXXy

eXcellent

eXcellent!

FoXXXY

Anchor	DMC
2	blanc
~ 334	606
☆ 306	783
128	775
1047	402
1048	3776
■ 403	310

French Knots: 403
Backstitch:
334—exclamation point
1005—"FoxxxY"
147/797—"eXcellent" (except "x") quotation mark
351/400—fox (except ears, eye, nose, mouth)
400/317—dog
403—fox's ears, eye, nose, mouth, purse, dress, zigzag line

Y is for...

Yippee!
Yak
Yak, Yak, Yak
Yarn
Yolks
Yawn

Anchor	DMC
2	blanc
305	743
128	775
130	809
881	945
1047	402
403	310

Backstitch:
351/400—bear (except
   eyes, nose)
400/317—shirt
403—eyes, nose, "Y"

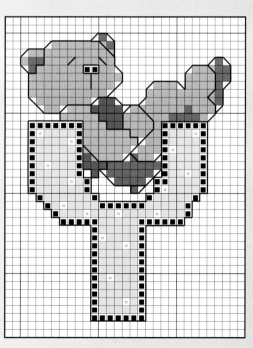

173

Anchor	DMC
387	712
24	963
881	945
1047	402

French Knots:
334/606—lettering
403/310—nose

Backstitch:
39/309—lower mouth
334—lettering
351/400—bear (except nose, mouth)
403—nose, mouth

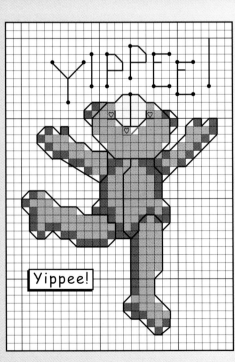

Yippee!

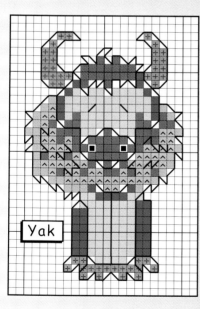

Yak

	Anchor	DMC
☐	387	712
▨	50	3716
▨	103	3609
⊞	311	676
▨	128	775
▨	130	809
⌃	342	211
▨	109	209
▨	881	945
▨	1047	402
■	403	310

French Knots:
162—lettering
403/825—eyes, noses
Backstitch:
162—lettering
351/400—bears (except
  noses, mouths)
400/317—yak (except eyes)
403—phones, bears' noses,
  yak's eyes

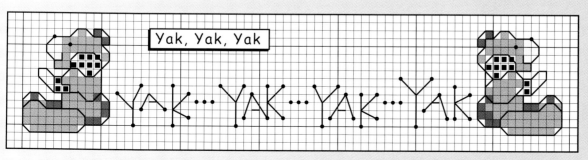

Yak, Yak, Yak

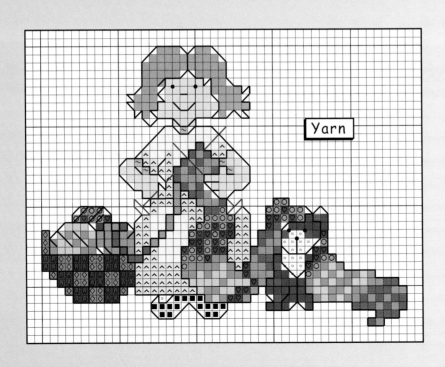

Yarn

Anchor	DMC
2	blanc
95	554
778	3774
868	758
323	722
292	3078
295	726
311	676
361	738
1092	964
186	959
128	775
130	809
109	209
366	951
347	402
403	310

French Knots: 403

Backstitch:

39/309—girl's mouth

334/606—needles

1013/3778—skin

162/825—left and middle
    yarn balls

110/208—right yarn ball,
    yarn strand

884/356—hair, cat (except
    nose), basket

400/317—dress, scarf

403—shoes, cat's nose

Anchor	DMC
2	blanc
387	712
334	606
305	743
203	564
128	775
103	3609
109	209
881	945
1047	402
234	762

French Knots: 403/310

Backstitch:
351/400—shelf, bear (except nose), hen's beak, yolks
400/317—hen, remaining eggs, clothes
403—nose

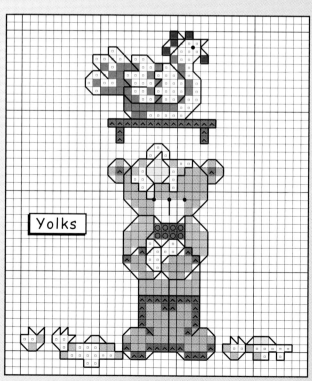

Yolks

Yawn

	Anchor	DMC
	387	712
	73	963
	75	962
	206	564
	204	563
	881	945
	1048	3776

French Knots: 403/310

Backstitch:

42/326—slippers (except noses)

205/912—pajama stripes

210/562—remaining pajamas

351/400—bear (except eyes, nose, mouth)

403/310—eyes, nose, mouth

Z is for...

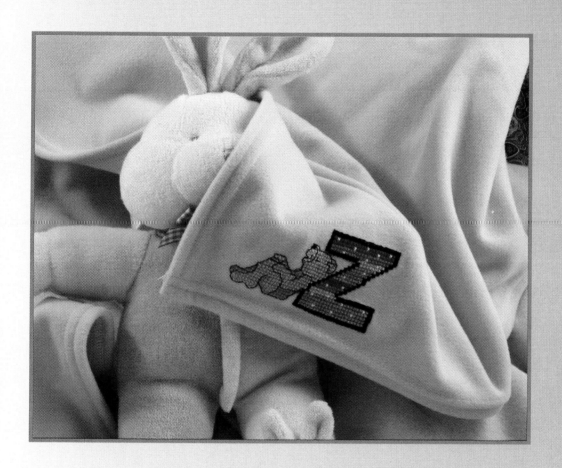

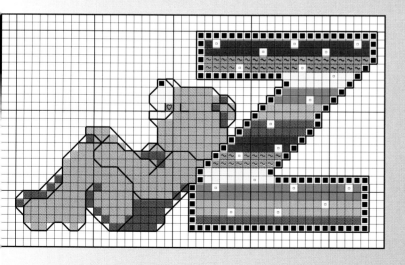

Anchor	DMC
2	blanc
387	712
24	963
334	606
329	3340
305	743
238	703
130	809
96	3609
881	945
1047	402
403	310

Backstitch:
351—bear (except
   eye, nose, mouth)
403—eye, nose,
   mouth, "Z"

Zoo

Anchor	DMC	Anchor	DMC	Backstitch:
2	blanc	211	562	351/400—giraffe (except eye, nostril, mouth, hooves), lion (except eyes, nose, mouth), bear (except eyes, nose, mouth), toucan's legs, penguin's beak & feet
50	3716	128	775	
52	957	130	809	
334	606	146	322	
303	742	143	324	
329	3340	95	554	
332	946	109	209	
295	726	110	208	
311	676	881	945	
253	472	1047	402	400/317—hippo (except eye), sign
238	703	1049	301	
206	564	399	318	403—remaining outlines
205	912	403	310	

Z is for...
Zebra   Zombie

Anchor	DMC
▫ 2	blanc
~ 334	606
▨ 1005	816
314	741
305	743
253	472
238	703
⊙ 185	964
128	775
△ 129	800
121	809
95	554
97	553
■ 403	310
Backstitch: 403	

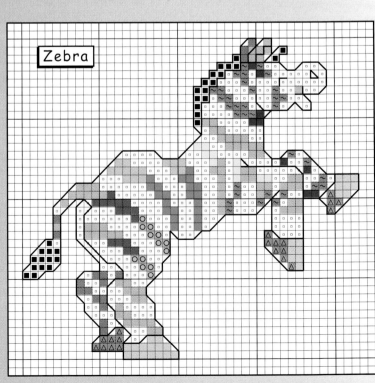

Zebra

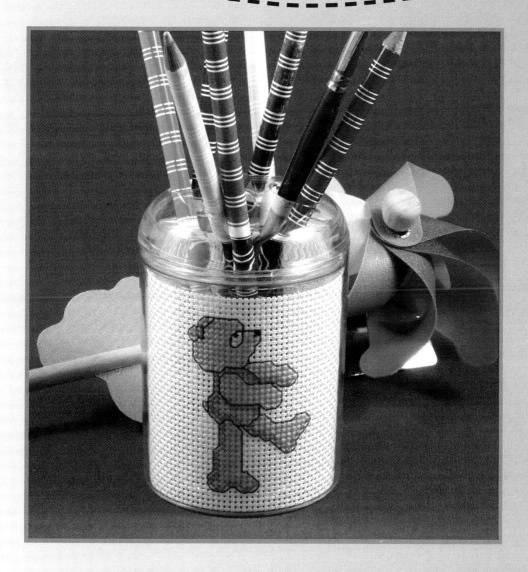

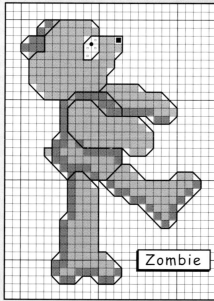

Anchor	DMC
2	blanc
881	945
1047	402
403	310

French Knot: 403
Backstitch:
351/400—bear
  (except nose)
403—nose

Zombie

Anchor	DMC
305	743
128	775
881	945
1047	402
398	415
■ 403	310

French Knots:
334/606—first two "Z"s
314/741—second two "Z"s
209/913—third two "Z"s
162/825—fourth two "Z"s
98/553—last two "Z"s
403—eyes, nose, antennae

Backstitch:
334—first two "Z"s
314—second two "Z"s
209—third two "Z"s
146/322—wings
162—fourth two "Z"s
147/797—dust clouds,
    motion lines, "ZOOM"
98—last two "Z"s
351/400—bear (except nose)
403—remaining bees, bear's
    nose

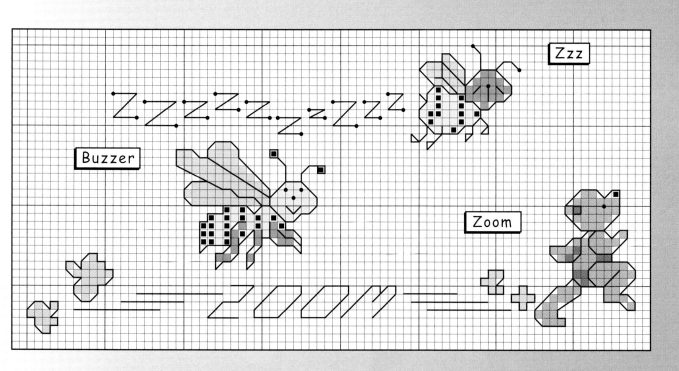

Z is for...
Zonked

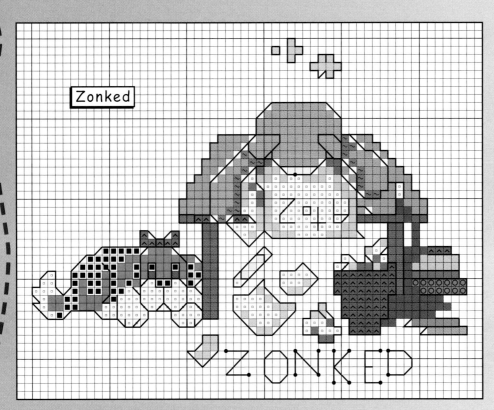

Zonked

Anchor	DMC
2	blanc
387	712
334	606
314	741
305	743
361	738
363	436
254	3348
225	703
128	775
130	809
96	3609
881	945
1047	402
351	400
399	318
403	310

French Knots:
43/814—lettering
403—bear's nose

Backstitch:
43—"ZONKED"
334—"A to Z," dog's bow, red pencil
245/986—green pencil
136/799—clouds
98/553—purple pencil
351/400—bear, yellow pencil
400/317—table, papers, basket, books, coffee cup
403—dog

General Directions

THE MATERIALS

The materials required for counted cross-stitch are few and inexpensive: a piece of evenweave fabric, a tapestry needle, some six-strand cotton floss, scissors, and a charted design. An embroidery hoop is optional. All of these products are readily available at needlework departments or shops.

Fabric

For counted cross-stitch embroidery we use "evenweave" fabrics which are woven with the same number of horizontal and vertical threads per inch. Cross-stitches are made over the intersections of the horizontal and vertical threads, and because the number of threads in each direction is equal, each stitch will be the same size and perfectly square. A fabric is described by the number of threads per inch; that number is called its thread count.

The thread count and the number of stitches will determine the finished size of a stitched design. Fabric with a higher thread count will produce a small design (more stitches are worked per inch) and a lower thread count will produce a larger design because there are fewer stitches per inch.

Evenweave fabrics commonly used for cross-stitch are Aida cloth, linen, an array of specialty fabrics, and waste canvas. There are also many kinds of pre-made evenweave products.

Aida Cloth is a cotton fabric that has groups of four threads woven in a basketweave pattern, making the intersections very easy to see. Aida is woven in several sizes, measured by the number of squares: 11-count (11 stitches per inch), 14-count, 16-count, and 18-count. The most commonly used Aida is 14-count.

Linen is woven of single threads. Cross-stitches are made over two threads in each direction. Linen may be a bit difficult for beginners to use, as there are no obvious intersections as on Aida, but a little practice will produce great results.

Linen is available in a variety of thread counts. Because the stitches are worked over two threads, the number of stitches per inch will be half the thread count. For example, on 28-count linen, you will work 14 stitches to the inch, the same finished size as if the design was worked on 14-count Aida.

Specialty Fabrics are woven in the same manner as linen, but may be cotton, synthetic, or a combination of fibers. These fabrics will have different thread counts and may be known by different names, depending on the manufacturer. There are also some **non-fabric surfaces** that are popular for counted cross stitch. Vinyl-Weave™ is a vinyl product that looks like Aida cloth, is waterproof, and does not ravel. Perforated paper is a pressed paper with small round holes and stitches are made over the spaces between the holes; it is somewhat fragile. Perforated plastic is a plastic canvas that looks like perforated paper but is structurally stronger.

Waste Canvas can be used if you wish to cross stitch on a non-evenweave surface, such as clothing. It is a temporary evenweave product that is available in a variety of thread counts. Baste a piece of waste canvas onto the surface to be cross stitched, work over the canvas threads, then remove the canvas threads after the stitching is complete.

Pre-finished Products are very convenient if you want to stitch a towel, pillow, or baby bib, but you don't like to sew. Most pre-made products, such as the towels and baby bib pictured here and on page 42, incorporate evenweave fabric (usually Aida) as part of their construction. These products have a pre-determined amount of space available for stitching. When working on pre-mades, be sure the design you select will fit on the product before you begin stitching.

Use the chart below as a guide to determine the approximate finished width and height of a stitched design based on the count of your chosen background fabric.

Thread Count	Number of Stitches in Design				
	10	20	30	40	50
11-count	1"	1¾"	2¾"	3⅝"	4½"
14-count	¾"	1⅜"	2⅛"	2⅞"	3⅝"
16-count	⅝"	1¼"	1⅞"	2½"	3⅛"
18-count	½"	1⅛"	1⅝"	2¼"	2¾"

(measurements are given to the nearest ⅛")

Threads

The most commonly used thread for counted cross-stitch is six-strand cotton embroidery floss. It can be divided to work with one, two, or more strands at a time. Separate the floss into individual strands, then put the required number back together before threading the needle.

Designs cross-stitched on 16-count Aida Cloth are stitched with two strands of floss.
The 16-count fabric allows the true color intensity to show. On 14-count fabrics, two strands of floss are usually used, but the color will be less intense because the background fabric is slightly visible. On 14-count perforated surfaces, three strands are recommended because the space over which the stitch is made is relatively small. On 18-count fabrics, one strand of floss is used.

Needles

A small blunt-tipped tapestry needle, size 24 or 26, is used for stitching. The higher the needle number, the smaller the needle. The correct size needle is fairly easy to thread with the amount of floss required, but not so large that it will distort the fabric. The chart below tells you which size needle is appropriate for each size of Aida cloth and suggests the number of floss strands to use.

Fabric	Stitches Per Inch	Strands of Floss	Tapestry Needle Size
Aida	11	3	22 or 24
Aida	14	2	24 or 26
Aida	16	2	24, 26 or 28
Aida	18	1 or 2	26 or 28

PLANNING YOUR PROJECT

You can work any of the designs alone as a small project, two or three as companion pieces, or you can combine similar designs to cover a larger surface. However you choose to use the designs, the planning process will be the same.

Select your chart and type of fabric or pre-finished product. Determine the finished dimensions of the stitched area. Divide the number of stitches in width by the number of stitches per inch of fabric. This tells you how many inches wide the design will be. Repeat for the height of the design. Or, for an approximate size, refer to the table.

If you are working an arrangement of several designs, or repeating the same design as shown on the hat band on page 72 and in the photo below, we recommend you draw the outlines, or mark outside dimensions, on a piece of graph paper before beginning to stitch.

General Directions (continued)

Add enough additional fabric for desired unworked area around the design plus an additional 2" or 3" on each side for use in finishing and mounting. If you are using a pre-made item, make sure there is a large enough stitching area available.

Cut your fabric exactly true, even with the weave. Some raveling may occur as you handle the fabric while stitching. To minimize raveling, along the raw edges use an overcast basting stitch, machine zigzag stitch, or masking tape (to be cut away when you are finished).

Ideally, the progression of your work should be from left to right and from the top of the design toward the bottom. With this sequence, you will bring your thread up from the back to the front through unoccupied fabric holes and will stitch down from front to back through already occupied holes, thereby disturbing completed stitches as little as possible.

GETTING STARTED

Cut floss into comfortable working lengths; we suggest about 18". To begin in an unstitched area, bring threaded needle to front of fabric. Hold an inch of the end against the back, then anchor it with your first few stitches. To end threads and begin new ones next to existing stitches, weave through the backs of several stitches.

Trim thread ends close to fabric. Wherever possible, end your thread under stitches of the same color and toward the center of the design.

THE STITCHES

Note: Use two strands of floss for all cross-stitches and one strand for backstitches, straight stitches, and French knots, unless otherwise noted in the color key.

Cross-Stitch

The cross-stitch is formed in two motions. Follow the numbering in **Fig 1** and bring needle up at 1, down at 2, up at 3, down at 4 to complete the stitch. Work horizontal rows of stitches, **Fig 2**, wherever possible. Bring thread up at 1, work half of each stitch across the row, then complete the stitches on your return.

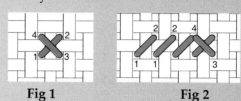

Fig 1   Fig 2

When a vertical row of stitches is appropriate for the design, complete each stitch then proceed to the next as shown in **Fig 3**. No matter how you work the stitches, make sure that all crosses slant in the same direction.

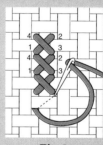

Fig 3

French Knot

Bring thread up where indicated on chart. Wrap floss once around needle, **Fig 4**, and reinsert needle at 2, close to 1, but at least one fabric thread away from it. Hold wrapping thread tightly and pull needle through, releasing thread just as knot is formed. For a larger knot, use more strands of floss, but wrap only once.

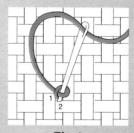

Fig 4

Occasionally, the color key will use colored dots to help differentiate the floss colors to be used.

189

Backstitch

Backstitches are worked after cross-stitches have been completed. They may slope in any direction and are occasionally worked over more than one square of fabric. **Fig 5** shows the progression of several stitches; bring thread up at odd numbers and down at even numbers.

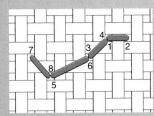

Fig 5

Frequently you must choose where to end one backstitch color and begin the next color. As a rule of thumb, choose the object that should appear closest to you. Backstitch around that shape with the appropriate color, then backstitch the areas behind it with adjacent color(s).

Occasionally, a color key will have two backstitch symbols (a thick line and a thin one), or colored lines to help you differentiate colors.

Straight Stitch

A straight stitch, **Fig 6**, is made like a long backstitch. Come up at one end of the stitch and down at the other. The length and direction of these stitches will vary—follow the chart for exact placement. Be sure to secure thread well at the beginning and ending of a group of straight stitches so they stay taut.

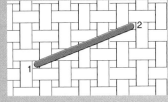

Fig 6

Eyelet

Bring thread up at any point along the outside of the charted shape, **Fig 7**, and stitch down into the center. Continue to work around the shape as shown on the chart always entering at center of eyelet.

Fig 7

FINISHING NEEDLEWORK

Most needleworkers love to stitch, but tend to get bogged down with the finishing process. It need not be so. While most projects are framed, there are many easy (and inexpensive) ways to finish your work, especially with these delightful designs.

When you have finished stitching, dampen your embroidery. If soiled, wash stitched fabric in cool water with a gentle soap. Rinse well. Roll in a towel and squeeze out excess moisture. Place face down on a dry towel or padded surface and iron carefully. Make sure all thread ends are well anchored and clipped closely.

PRE-FINISHED PRODUCTS

We have shown a variety of easy finishing products on our photographed models. We've used pre-finished bibs, towels, bookmarks, and other ready-to-stitch items. Some designs are stitched directly onto clothing using waste canvas. Many others are stitched on a variety of fabrics, then inserted into small frames or cups made for this purpose. Fabric with pre-finished edgings can be glued around canning jars or around photo albums. Most of these items are available at your local craft and needlework stores.

You will find a large variety of mounting boards and decorative frames available for do-it-yourself framing, or you may choose to have samplers and other intricate designs professionally framed.

GIFT IDEAS

Cross-stitch designs are an excellent way to give something special. As you choose items for a new baby, or purchase a t-shirt for a friend, think of ways to embellish your gift—with the touch of an added design stitched by you. Add initials to towels and table linens. Hang tiny framed ornaments on Christmas trees, or tie them with ribbon on gift boxes. Gift ideas are endless when you allow your imagination to soar.